Praise for Coming of Age with Aging Parents . . .

"Excellent! Highly recommended reading for caregivers and for everyone who may eventually need one."

–Jacqueline Marcell
Author of *Elder Rage, or Take My Father . . . Please!*

"A heartwarming, humorous, and eminently helpful look at the roller-coaster journey of eldercare. I wish my siblings and I had this treasure to guide us when we accompanied our parents on the final leg of their earthly journey."

–Jim Shaw, M.D.
Medical director, Providence Center for Faith and Healing

"*Coming of Age with Aging Parents* is alive with heart, humor, insight, and creative solutions. Drawing from her unique personal experience, Goeller offers invaluable guidance and shows us the immense potential for personal growth and fulfillment that comes when we open to the grand adventure of supporting our elders."

–Marilyn Mitchell
Author of *Dancing on Quicksand*

"One of Goeller's many gifts is finding the 'life lesson' in the most mundane situations. In *Coming of Age with Aging Parents,* she shares those life lessons in a way that builds confidence and inspires hope. She has taken what could certainly be called great challenges, added a light touch of humor, and educated us all on the issues we will face. This book serves as a 'heads up' for what can come, as well as a handbook for tackling each situation as it arises. It should be read and reread."

–Anne Koepsell
Board member, Washington State Hospice & Palliative Care Organization

Coming of Age
with
Aging Parents

The
Bungles,
Battles,
and
Blessings

GAIL GOELLER

PATINA PRODUCTIONS
Spokane, Washington

Published by:

PATINA PRODUCTIONS
PO BOX 20031
SPOKANE, WA 99204

Editor: Ellen Kleiner
Cover art: Melissa Magnuson
Book design and typography: Angela Werneke

Printed in the United States of America on acid-free recycled paper

Publisher's Cataloging-in-Publication Data

Goeller, Gail.
    Coming of age with aging parents : the bungles, battles, and
    blessings / Gail Goeller. – 1st ed. – Spokane, WA : Patina
    Productions, 2004.

        p. ; cm.

        Includes bibliographical references.
        ISBN: 0-9746338-0-1

        1. Aging parents–Care. 2. Aged–Care. 3. Aged–
    Family relationships. I. Title.

HQ755.86 .G64 2004   2003097497
306.874–dc22   0404

10 9 8 7 6 5 4 3 2 1

To John ~
my husband and eldercare partner in horizontal time,
cheerleader, and clarifier,
from whom I borrowed confidence
to pen this history

And to my loving, funny, profound, and creative parents,
Cart and Jeanne

In Gratitude ————

I am grateful to the earthly angels of Hospice of Spokane, who taught and inspired me, all the while bundling my family with love.

Thanks to my brothers and sisters-in-law, Kip and Bev Gladder and Ed and Kelly Gladder, for hanging in there, especially Kip, who lent me his "caring from a distance" lenses.

Thanks also to our children, Greg and Patti Goeller and Kaaren and Bill Bloom, who stitched adoration into the seams of their grandparents' fading fabric; to Jonas Gregory and Lucas Carlton Goeller, and Ava Gail Bloom, for lightening our losses with a new generation of candles; to the many people who listened, read, commiserated, laughed, and spilled tears with me along the way; to our family's dear friends Brian and Betty O'Donnell and to our many relatives, particularly Jim and Jackie Wade, Jane Butkay, and Seleta Austin, who never let us out of their sight throughout our twelve years in the trenches of eldercare.

I am further grateful to the professionals who generously padded the trail of this book at various junctures: writers M.E. Buckham, Dorothy Fredericks, Bryan Harnetiaux, and Debbie Lockhert, all early encouragers; street-smart Donita Basinger, Laura L. Bracken, Ruth Fearn, Deb Kellerman, Anne Koepsell, Deb Strauss, and Becky Tiller, who kindly offered their eldercare expertise; author Marilyn Mitchell, my you-can-count-on-honest-feedback coach; Lisa Lucas, a canine goddess who deepened my appreciation for elders and pets; artist Louise Kodis for providing a personally designed writer's nook; and author Linda Hagen Miller, a Renaissance woman who stepped out of nowhere to walk by my side.

Finally, thanks to Ellen Kleiner, my faithful, brilliant, and gifted editor and guide.

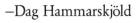

Life only demands from you the strength you possess. . . .
Only one feat is possible—not to have run away.

—Dag Hammarskjöld

Contents

Part 2: HANGING ON

Part 3: LETTING GO

Part 4: FAMILY AFFAIRS

Preface

In May 1990, my husband John and I each extinguished forty-six candles in commemoration of our birthdays, wishing for a simpler future. It seemed a reasonable request since our son and daughter were attending college and preparing for the wider life, our careers—mine as a management consultant and John's as an educator—were flourishing, and our marriage was stable. As "kids who returned home" to Spokane, Washington, we lived in both the shadow and embrace of our families. Yes, our parents were aging, but they were so self-sufficient. Except for an occasional call for help from one of them, our days were flavored with a dram of comfort and a measure of peace.

The truth was that we were sailing through life so rapidly we ignored the storm warnings. When John's father died the following fall, we abruptly grounded on a snag that woke us up to what really was happening with our aging parents. Subsequently, John's mother provided our rite of passage into full-blown eldercare, changing our lives forever. Accustomed to a strict division of labor like many who married in the early 1940s, after her husband died she could not manage her own finances, required alternative transportation, and needed ongoing assistance maintaining her seventy-year-old home. It was in 1992, when she was diagnosed with Alzheimer's disease, that we were forced to face the many challenges and dilemmas associated with eldercare. The more we strained to create rhythm and meaning in her life and ours, the more we flailed in crisis management. Suddenly, we were not only grieving the death of John's father but also mourning the loss of his mother to dementia.

Then further loss loomed. In January 1993, my seventy-three-year-old mother sustained a major stroke and died two months later, leaving behind my father, who was eleven years her senior.

Although mentally alert, he was overcome with grief and had a strong desire to stay in the family home, so we helped him whenever necessary. A month later, when it became apparent John's aunt could no longer live without assistance, we moved her into my mother-in-law's home.

We were now simultaneously trying to keep one elder with Alzheimer's from escaping home, while getting her sister settled into it, as well as propping up my feisty father to avoid having to dynamite him out of his quarters. Over the next twelve years we continued to care for our elders until the last one, my father, died at age ninety-two.

During this period of overwhelm, we only realized we would survive once we had begun to laugh. We hunted humor, finding it in unexpected places. We cackled when the sisters unwittingly traded false teeth. We howled when my dad foiled our attempts to relieve him of his car. We hooted day after day until we had cracked open a space big enough to allow for peace and healing in the midst of eldercare. With the wider perspective gained through humor, we quit our jobs and, leaving the safety net of our careers, trusted we would be taken care of just as we intended to care for our elders.

Hindsight has since granted us glimpses into our growth as a result of our twelve-year sojourn in eldercare. Characterized by bungles and battles, our transition to eldercare lacked polish, but eventually we managed to maneuver through adult rites of passage that altered our sense of self, family, and the place of humankind in a vast universe. Along the way we released the myth of being in charge, learning that each family member had a path separate from ours with its own connection to the greater good and that we were present in their lives only to facilitate the unfolding of their fate. Ultimately, we deepened our faith, reconfigured our value systems, and surged with gratitude for the opportunity to interact with our elders before it was too late. We discovered new ways to relate to siblings and other relatives, as well, rising above rivalry to focus on the common goals of caregiving.

Throughout these years of eldercare, our children cheered us on, often participating, in their unique ways. Only later did we realize they may have been previewing scenarios that would occur in the twilight of their own parents' lives.

While this book chronicles many of our personal dilemmas as caregivers, the tales have been universalized to inform and encourage any adult child who, despite hopes of an uncomplicated future, is suddenly faced, as if by firelight in a cave, with the realities of eldercare. As such, it presents not only the problems but the often hidden rewards awaiting those who take up this responsibility. Each section focuses on a particular aspect of eldercare and includes questions to consider for deepening the inner experience of caregiving. Resources incorporated at the end of the book further clarify potential problems that might arise. Throughout, humor is injected—not to deny the seriousness of eldercare issues but as a therapeutic tool to help in gaining perspective and healing.

Introduction ————

Today, millions of adult children are being called to invest in their own stock: aging parents. As a new commodity in the rites-of-passage industry, the eldercare venture initially appears inconvenient, scaring off many potential speculators. However, when allowed to mature, it pays a formidable dividend called coming of age.

Rarely is tending to our parents on the calendar until we are confronted with events that force us to face such a possibility. Sometimes a parent's previously ignored patterns of self-neglect or dementia reach critical mass. Other times, one parent becomes very ill or suddenly dies, and we watch the other flounder, bereft of skills necessary to carry on.

The timing of such events can be exasperatingly inopportune, occurring, perhaps, the very week a rebellious teen has sent us scuttling to therapy, or just when we've agreed to care for a grandchild or launch a second career. Accustomed to viewing our parents' problems as temporary, we juggle our schedule and pledge to layer in eldercare without giving up our lifestyle or other commitments. Before long, however, we discover that caring for an aging parent requires uncompromising measures of endurance, sacrifice, and teamwork.

Then, too, from the periphery eldercare may appear as a selfless service calling for a level of involvement we can control. But we are apt to find it a developmental fire hydrant that, bursting through heartbreak, causes us to reassess both our role in the family and our identity. Like any rite of passage, parental caregiving entails pain and suffering. There is simply no lighthearted way to move parents out of the family home, help mediate their cancer diagnosis, deal with their dementia, or curtail their independence as their capacities are diminished.

Nor does either proximity or distance ease the anguish. If parents live nearby, we may feel lucky to have their companionship yet resentful about shouldering the burden of care; if they live far away, we may feel less pressured but guilty about neglecting them. Wherever we are along the continuum of involvement, we are bound to experience ambiguity and powerlessness.

Eldercare poses unforeseen challenges in a culture significantly more well-versed in childhood development. Whereas a child progresses from dependence to independence, an elder does the opposite, forcing us to constantly contract our perspective, expectations, and strategies. Some decisions will be brilliant, such as designating our role as "housekeeper" rather than "caregiver." Others may be disastrous, such as waiting too long to take away the car keys. If you have siblings, eldercare may trigger family conflicts, or a surfacing of unfinished business. With luck, unavoidable clashes will be resolved while your parents are still alive; should fate intervene, consider reaching out to forces beyond the physical world to gain perspective and inner strength.

Although parental caregiving can cause strife and stress, it advances our growth toward wholeness. While caring for aging parents, we strengthen our bonds with them and other family members, trade in monologue for dialogue in a stretch toward intimacy, and activate desirable qualities and behaviors we never knew we had. Surprising opportunities along the way open windows to the sweetness of love, a deepened sense of purpose, an enhanced understanding of the life cycle, and an increased ability to show compassion for humanity.

Coming of Age with Aging Parents: The Bungles, Battles, and Blessings is not an instructional guide but an educational lens for viewing thought-provoking scenarios involving eldercare under various conditions. Use the book to explore caregiving options, stimulate intergenerational dialogue about end-of-life planning, shift your state of mind, and unlock the saving grace of laughter. Above all, allow vignettes mirroring your situations with an aging parent to inspire action grounded in purpose and a heart open despite trauma.

When a crisis arises concerning a parent's health or safety, do your best to not react. Instead, educate yourself about the circumstance and possible courses of action, consulting your parent and perhaps professionals or select family members as well. If you are spiritually inclined, you may also want to reflect or pray before acting. With purposeful actions and an expansive heart, you can negotiate nearly any crisis and simultaneously transform it into a personal rite of passage. Using this approach, many individuals who commence the eldercare journey as children, lacking the perspective and capacity for dealing with its unique challenges, emerge as more caring and stronger adults.

This journey has no easy answers. If you have fallen under the spell of quick solutions, invest in a pair of waders for the inevitable moments of wallowing in an eldercare river of no return. To keep from drowning, stay open to possibilities rather than fixating prematurely on some "right" way. Part of coming of age is getting comfortable with trial and error as a means of discovering innovative resolutions for desperate situations. The questions at the end of each vignette provide opportunities for accessing the knowledge of your heart rather than focusing only on practical answers. As you reflect on the mysteries in your life and share your discoveries with other family members or a support group of peers, solutions will eventually emerge. But even these may need to be altered when circumstances change once again.

The book's segments trace the course of the adult child's gradual unfolding. Part 1, "Wake-Up Calls," focuses on events signaling the need for eldercare and effective ways of accepting it. Part 2, "Hanging On," exposes the caregiver's need for control in the midst of unpredictability. Part 3, "Letting Go," deals with ways of relinquishing control to gain freedom and prepare for personal development. Part 4, "Family Affairs," portrays rich insights that can emerge from the confrontation of such potentially volatile subjects as money and favoritism. Finally, Part 5, "Higher Altitudes," charts trails to a summit of faith, hope, and gratitude, providing new perspectives on growth from the eldercare experience.

PART 1 ——
Wake-Up Calls

Sudden confrontations with the reality of a parent's decline can be terrifying and heart wrenching. A typical scenario might be the following. In the midst of a supercharged day, the phone rings and you strain to hear the barely audible voice, finally realizing it's your parent dialing from a pay phone on the corner of Mortal and Finite, with an urgent message: they need help.

On the game board of inevitability, they rolled the dice, and their chip has landed on chronic disease, financial crisis, a death in the family, sudden incapacity or dementia, or problems with housing or transportation. Skating between disbelief and panic, you wake up to a harsh reality: while you were busy ascending, Mom or Dad was descending. And you are doubly alarmed because you have not planned ahead for contingencies.

For me and my husband John, the wake-up call concerned a death in the family, a crisis immediately followed by clusters of lesser emergencies that pulled us back into our aging parents' fold. By the time we had acknowledged crumbling homesteads, survived two bathroom catastrophes, heeded a final warning from the IRS regarding unpaid taxes, and confiscated a loaded gun, we were into eldercare up to our eyeballs, overwhelmed by the challenges yet also amazed by our sense of mission.

If you get a wake-up call about the declining status of a parent, first orient yourself by asking some fundamental questions, such as:

- Why is this problem occurring?
- Are all the necessary people involved?
- Is there anyone from whom you need to gather more information?
- What is your intuition telling you?
- What is your plan for solving the problem?

Then reach out for assistance, recording your questions and trusting answers will come once you have enlisted help. During the outreach phase, expect immediate rewards: the vernacular of eldercare will expand your vocabulary, and the renewal of bonds with long-distance family members will keep you steeped in tribal lore. You may also need to engage your parent in discussions about topics that have been avoided till now, exposing yourself to reactions of directness one day and silence or aloofness the next while your parent grapples with vulnerabilities about their future. As you attempt to understand the social and financial services available to your parent, confusion may set in, but eventually the fog will lift. Some of the best advice will probably come from unlikely sources—such as a seasoned caregiver at a checkout counter who overhears your tribulations and shares their story.

While gathering knowledge and advice, remember that your best-made plans can change over time and that your ability to adapt to the resulting shifts is as important as ascertaining information for making key decisions. It may also help to recall the saying "Fall down seven times, stand up eight." The following vignettes and questions explore scenarios that announce the need for eldercare and point the way to solutions.

It's Nearly Midnight,
Do You Know Where Your Parents Are?

Though hectic, your midlife has a satisfying rhythm. Then the calls for help, random accidents, and personality changes begin. An unsettled feeling signs a lease agreement with your gut.

The ringing phone forced my husband out of a deep sleep. His mother Impie, who lived alone across town, was calling to report that she couldn't turn off the shower. "It's a stheady sthream," she bellowed, obviously bereft of her false teeth.

John glanced at the clock's digital glow. "Hey, what are you doing in the shower at midnight?"

Impie made a U-turn back to her quandary, wailing, "I can't shut off the water. What am I gonna do?"

Blinking himself awake, John instructed, "Try it again while I hang on." Listening to her pad toward the bathroom, he muttered to himself, "Last week it was her neighbor calling to say she's wandering in circles around her kitchen, and yesterday I had to haul in the living room furniture she'd piled on the porch. Geez, am I going to need to move back home?"

"It's sthill a stheady sthream," Mom howled.

Resigned, John dragged himself out from beneath the down comforter, dressed, and drove to her home. Discovering she had stripped the threads on both faucets, he shut down the water system and made a mental note to call a plumber in the morning. Then he headed back for a few more hours of sleep, quickly converting his worries about her well-being into respect for the legitimacy of her call.

After Mom's third "shower hour" incident, we sought a medical diagnosis, so we could hear out loud what we had silently suspected—she probably had Alzheimer's disease. In addition to our immediate concern for her well-being, we were stunned to discover the plethora of symptoms we had previously ignored, no doubt out of denial. We also had to confess our greatest fear: that John's mother would become completely dependent on us, altering our lives. Although this fear was ultimately realized, the effects on our family were much more complex than we had imagined, involving not only trials but also transcendence.

If you are secretly concerned about a parent's mental health . . .

If your parent's mental capacity is deteriorating, it may be time for a definitive prognosis. To assess the situation, look for preambles to dementia, such as the inability to locate a number in the telephone directory, the tendency to defer to others when asked to make personal decisions, or involvement in a fender bender because "the sun was in my eyes" when actually the road led due north, away from the sun.

For added confirmation, explore the following questions:

- Have you noticed recent changes in your parent's behavior? Does your parent share these perceptions?

- Are you cognizant of any past medical conditions or family history that points to dementia?

- Given your parent's age and health status, would a geriatric assessment be desirable, if only to substantiate or negate your observations?

——— COMING OF AGE PASSAGE ———
Facing denial

Damage Control with Duct Tape

When your parent's home maintenance gets casual and creative, beware!

Whether the finish on the dining room table needed a facelift or the roof required repair, my father Cart's lifelong response was, "I'm not going to pay someone to come and do work I can do myself." Though he lacked sufficient talent to perform most home-maintenance tasks, he was strong on stubbornness and determination. Through the years, his ventures in pounding, cutting, plugging, and wrapping had warded off disaster. As he aged, however, his handyman tactics became increasingly precarious.

For instance, while I was pushing the dust mop around my parents' vinyl living room floor one morning, I happened upon a snarl of home-brewed electrical confusion. It appeared that Dad, though in the early stages of glaucoma, considered himself competent to attend to the house's wiring. Looking further, I saw that instead of wiring an outdoor sensor light into a circuit breaker Dad had run a long, frayed extension cord patched with duct tape over the garden and through a window near an outlet, increasing the potential not only for a house fire but for an intruder's ease of entry.

Conferring, my brother Kip and I recalled how duct tape had always been Dad's favored means of propping up the old homestead. On one of his visits, my brother encountered a small lake on our parents' kitchen floor and, upon inspecting the plumbing underneath the sink, spotted the silver adhesive swathing a joint that suffered from metal psoriasis. Dad had also used duct tape for mending garden hoses, wrapping cracked handles on tools, binding weakened bed frames, reinforcing window insulation, and reattaching the deck carpet.

Across town, John's father Ray had undertaken similar home improvement projects. One day John had walked in on his father heating a can of slightly dried paint on a stove burner. When John divulged his fear of an explosion, Ray assured him the control was set to the lowest temperature.

On a cold winter morning when the furnace was distributing heat disproportionately throughout his parents' house, John noticed the oven door had been opened to warm up the kitchen. Ray explained it was a practice he had reinstated from his youth.

In addition, the standard strategy for dealing with leaky faucets at John's parents' house was to dig through a coffee tin jam-packed with washers in an attempt to match the problem faucet. This method usually resulted in a faulty repair, causing even more leakage.

After reflecting on these and other do-it-yourself projects, John and I were scared about the possible consequences, especially since our parents were now aging and less equipped to cope with disasters. We also recognized the importance of more frequent visits and, when necessary, interventions.

If your parent's home-maintenance strategies seem unsafe . . .

Become more observant of repairs and potentially hazardous conditions in your parent's home. For example, be aware of such things as a parent using a rickety dining room chair to change a porch light, replacing a lightbulb with a wattage that exceeds the lamp's guidelines, charring baking dishes, or accumulating stacks of old magazines and newspapers, causing a possible fire hazard. If you notice several such incidents, reassess your parent's judgment and abilities. In sharing your apprehensions, don't be surprised if your parent dismisses your concerns, becomes defensive, or gets sneaky. Older people often relax their former standards out of an uncompromising desire to remain in their homes, a need to feel in control of their environments, or an encroaching weariness of life-long tasks. But threats to their security might also signify judgment that isn't as good as it used to be or an unawareness of changes that have occurred.

As you raise safety issues with your parents, prepare for battles over components of a safe living situation. If clashes erupt, remember that conflict between generations is normal and can lead just as easily to better communication and closer connections as it can to estrangement.

If you become troubled while looking objectively at your parent's coping styles, your toughest job will be balancing your concerns with their dignity and independence—a theme that will dominate your eldercare experience. In situations warranting discussion or action, consider the following questions:

- Are your concerns about a parent's safety legitimate or exaggerated?

- Are you inviting your parent to participate in decisions affecting their life or are you attempting to take over the decision-making?

- How will you know if your parent is suffering from overwhelm or impaired judgment? If you sense danger, what measures can you take to ensure your parent's well-being?

——— COMING OF AGE PASSAGE ———
Objectifying your observations

Rub-a-Dub-Dub,
Grandma's Stuck in the Tub

Your aging parent insists she has no need for grab bars in the shower or tub, and you trust her assessment. Then she has an "episode," and it is clear that to continue her bathing activities she requires much more than equipment.

At age ninety-two, my grandmother still lived independently in her three-story home in Seattle, Washington, 260 miles from the closest family member, having managed her elder years with grace and unencumbered by fires, falls, or victimization by scam artists. By all accounts, she remained physically, emotionally, and mentally intact, an achievement due perhaps to traversing two flights of stairs each day or ingesting doses of ginkgo biloba. But one Sunday morning Mom got a call. It seems that on Friday evening Grandma had settled into her tub for a soak. Twenty minutes later she attempted to hoist herself to her knees, but her withered muscles failed, and she was stuck. There she sat, draining cold water and replacing it with warm each time the temperature dropped. At first she considered signaling for help, but she realized that hollering or banging would only sap energy.

The second morning of Grandma's marinade, a neighbor noticed two newspapers on the porch next door. After getting no response from a phone call as well as knocks on Grandma's door, the neighbor dialed 911. When the paramedics discovered a puckered Grandma in her claw-foot tub, thirty-four hours had passed. Swaddling her in terry cloth, they spotted a message she had etched on the tile with a bar of soap. Preparing for the worst, Grandma had written: "At least I got out clean!"

If your aging parent professes to be doing just fine on their own . . .

Most of us pray that our loved ones will live into old age

autonomously and in good health, succumbing to a quick death with little or no suffering. Unfortunately, only 25 percent of today's elders have such an experience. The remainder usually struggle through a prolonged illness, or some unforeseen accident snatches their independence.

Hoodwinked by wishful thinking, it is easy to take your parent's well-being for granted and thus miss signs that their health is deteriorating. To evaluate the need for precautionary measures, such as regular health assessments and safety checks, when an elder insists they are hardy and fit, ponder the following questions:

- Is it time to get second opinions about how your parent is really faring by seeking information from their friends, neighbors, or medical professionals?

- Has your parent established a way to signal neighbors if help is needed, such as determining a time when the kitchen shade will be pulled up each day to communicate all is well?

- So your parent can secure help whenever necessary, would it be wise to outfit them with an emergency response system (ERS), such as a button-operated signaling device in the form of a necklace or bracelet?

——— COMING OF AGE PASSAGE ———
Learning from crisis

If He Should Die Before I Wake

As well as you think you know your aging parent, there is a chance you aren't hearing the full story.

When my dad "robbed the cradle" at age thirty and captured Mom's nineteen-year-old heart, he knew what he was doing. Despite later financial hardship, career disappointment, and personality changes, they were still crazy about each other. But shortly after commemorating their fiftieth anniversary, a touch of marital strife began surfacing. Mom would mumble, "He's driving me crazy," while Dad forbade her to open her mouth until he had tossed the morning newspaper in the recycling bin because her "yakking" made it impossible for him to concentrate. Though they had withstood the usual amount of bickering over the years, including the often perilous transition into retirement, this new friction eventually seemed to threaten their cohabiting comfort levels. They were on each other's cases constantly while not sheltered in a solitary refuge—Mom in the garden, Dad in his den.

Reflecting on how they had arrived at this juncture, I realized that within one year Mom had blown kisses over both of her parents' graves. Though she had long been the matriarch of our clan, neither her children nor grandchildren needed her in ways they had when they were young. My brothers lived far away, while John and I now had professional lives that ate up the time we weren't with our children. In contrast to earlier years, when we regularly socialized with our parents, we had spread our wings and associated more with our own generation.

In addition, Mom had two dear friends with cancer and another with heart disease, as well as several longtime neighbors who had recently chosen to upgrade their lifestyles by relinquishing their older homes for suburbia. Whereas our kitchen had been the morning gathering place for the neighborhood's young mothers and toddlers, now Mom started the day by fixing herself and Dad a single cup of instant coffee. Nor was she able to utilize her homemaker talents, since her arthritic fingers curled up like cup hooks. Once her God-given genius as a seamstress had faltered, she became quietly frustrated, making "patience" her mantra while struggling with her identity. She seemed to be facing her own mortality.

She was further agitated by Dad's worries and disappointments. As a former state legislator, he had been accustomed to taking phone calls from people soliciting his opinion on referendums, but now the phone seldom rang. His golf game languished even more. As a result of all these circumstances, Dad's behavior had reverted to that of an only child intent on organizing his world primarily around himself, while Mom's fertile void was filled with question marks and despair.

Normally very social, Mom now isolated herself, not understanding her can't-live-with/can't-live-without predicament with her husband. Seeing Dad as her last link to security, she obsessed about her future, fearing what might happen to her if he should die first. Mom's apprehension became evident when our daughter, Kaaren, home for a college break, repeated a conversation she'd had with her grandmother. Amidst a torrent of tears, Mom had asked if she could come live with her granddaughter should Papa die. Caught by surprise, Kaaren had replied, "Grandma, I don't know how that would work exactly, but I bet we could figure something out." Her disclosure revealed the most accurate picture yet of my mother's emotional state.

Ultimately I realized that my mother, like many women her age, was so devoted to caregiving she had no idea how to ask for help of her own. She felt that if Dad should die before her, she would be forced to either learn his tasks in the marriage or ask for assistance—neither of which seemed likely to her. Equally futile were attempts made during my assertive woman stage to transfer my new value system to Mom. Even when her hair had grown over her eyebrows and blouse collars, she would not ask me to cut it.

Later, when Mom had a stroke, two surprises dismantled her expectations. First, she found that her anxiety about being left alone was probably unwarranted since it now appeared she would be exiting the earth plane before Dad, who ultimately outlived her by nine years. She also discovered that in times of need we children would vigilantly care for her.

If you suspect your parent has concerns about fending for themselves should they lose their partner. . .

If a parent begins demonstrating relationship behaviors mired in conflict, or suddenly starts withdrawing from you and others, examine the situation as neutrally as possible. Welcome input from your siblings, partner, or children, and try to open channels of communication with your parent. To gain further insight into the situation, consider the following questions:

- Have you invited your parent to talk about personal concerns, leading with a face-saving opener such as, "If I were you, I might be feeling . . ."?
- Are there signs your parent is experiencing marital discomfort?
- Have you contemplated the reality of one parent dying before the other and how that might impact the surviving parent?
- Do you know of useful resources your parent could call upon for help with marital problems or anxiety about being left alone after the death of their partner?

———— COMING OF AGE PASSAGE ————

Broadening your perspective on your parent's primary relationship

"What Is the IRS Going to Do with an Eighty-Eight-Year-Old Man?"

You assume your parent's financial affairs are under control until you discover they have put themselves in economic jeopardy.

Because Dad had managed the family's financial affairs since marrying my mother in 1940 and we considered him lucid in both speech and action, my brothers and I felt confident he was handling his money judiciously. We took it as a good sign when at the beginning of each month he complained about the cost of utilities and triumphed over the growth of his investments. "Crimany, they've raised the price of electricity again," he'd snort. "My Pfizer stock moved up three dollars a share," he'd gloat.

But our optimism about Dad's financial proficiency was shattered when we began encouraging him to give up his car. After explaining that the savings in car insurance would more than cover the cost of cabs or public transportation, we were shocked to hear him say, "Well, I haven't had car insurance since your mother died. They wanted to charge me nearly the same amount for just one of us, so I canceled the policy."

"Dad, you can't do that," I said. "If you were to have an accident, it could wipe out everything you've saved, including funds you might need for long-term care."

"Won't happen to me," he barked.

Antennae extended, I began inspecting his record-keeping system, discovering it was a little ragged around the edges. In fact, the file cabinet in which he had formerly stored financial documents was empty, and his invoices and receipts were in stacks atop a desk. Leafing through a pile, I was distressed to come upon a "Request for Tax Payment" form from the IRS stating that he was delinquent for the previous year. Underneath it were two warnings: "According to our records, you owe $443 on your income tax–please pay the full amount by November 8, 1999" and "Important Notice About Backup Withholding: If you don't pay the amount you owe, we may notify your bank or other payers to begin or continue backup withholdings. They will withhold 31 percent of your interest and/or dividend payments."

Recalling an earlier episode when Dad had been summoned for a tax audit, I was not surprised at his apparent disregard for the IRS notice. At that time, his antigovernment tactic was to cram a cardboard box with every bit of paperwork for the year, scramble its contents, and cart it to the federal building, where he sat poised in a chair amenable to answering questions posed by the auditor.

As the interrogation began, the federal employee requested specifics. "I notice you have taken a sizable medical deduction for the year. Are there canceled checks or invoices you can show me?" he asked.

Dad nodded in compliance. "Yes, I'm sure they are all here. Just give me a moment." He proceeded to present one paper after another, declaring each time, "Oh, I bet this is it. No, no, I guess not." An hour into the audit with several questions remaining, the investigator excused Dad and waived the penalties.

Now Dad proudly confessed he had been getting such notices from the IRS for several years, rationalizing, "What are they going to do to an eighty-eight-year-old man? Put me in jail? I'll outlast them. And when I die, they can't get my money. Simple as that."

On the verge of developing a full body rash, I blurted out, "Maybe you won't be around to deal with it, Dad, but your kids will!" I shuddered thinking of the research I'd have to do to substantiate his buying and selling piddling amounts of stock, let alone the dividends he had accrued.

"Look, if they come after you, just tell them you had no idea about my affairs. You guys will go nuts if you try to figure this out," he offered. I felt angry with Dad for the time it would take to unravel this mess and upset with myself for not uncovering his scheme sooner.

By the time we had become aware of Dad's mismanagement of finances, it was too late to do anything but painstakingly reconstruct his affairs. After explaining the situation to the IRS, I received an application for a "centralized authorization file" and, as Dad's power of attorney, was granted permission to take over his account with the Department of the Treasury. During this correspondence, an eighteen-page computer printout arrived itemizing Dad's failures to comply over the past five years. Finally, I gathered records from the three sources of his retirement income for the years of undisclosed income and contacted his bankers for any accrued interest. From his three brokers and a few companies with whom Dad had dealt independently, I was able to retrieve most of the prices at which he had bought and sold stock.

In the end, Dad owed the IRS only $576, but I had invested about twenty-seven hours of my time, not counting the distraction quotient causing an inability to focus on other aspects of my life. Cognizant of the crisis he had created, Dad handed over his checkbook, added my name to his accounts, and meek as a sheep, arranged for third-party notification of late payments.

If you are concerned about how well your parent is managing finances . . .

If you believe your parent has the potential to mismanage finances, it is wise to discuss money issues with them before the situation gets out of hand. To determine your role in helping to oversee their finances if intervention becomes necessary, consider the following questions:

- Is your parent receptive to sharing financial information and future economic plans with you?

- Are you willing to become educated in the legal and financial ramifications of your parent's current and future economic status?

- How will you know if your parent's ability to handle money is faltering? Where can you get information or advice concerning management of their finances?

———— COMING OF AGE PASSAGE ————
Seeing your parent through new eyes

"I Can't Get a Word in Edgewise!"

Businesses and care providers pride themselves on their "customer service" policies, but your parent may be reaping few such rewards.

Seniors are often adversely impacted by complicated systems, technologically challenging devices, or lack of sensitivity on the part of professionals who fail to take elders' problems into account. For example, on Dad's first solo flight to the cardiologist's office, feedback from the physician bolstered his ambition to reach a ripe old age, but upon departing he nearly died trying to locate his car. Though the parking spaces at the medical facility were assigned numerically, they were all painted the same color and each level was divided into two ramps, confusing even to a younger person with an acute sense of direction.

Honoring his promise to call me after returning home, Dad recounted, "I'm doing fine. Good report, considering. But I wore my legs out and was gasping for air in the parking lot. Thank God some older gentleman who had had the same experience took pity and volunteered to chauffeur me around until we found my car."

A month later, I joined Dad for his eye examination. Usually I respected his independence by waiting in the lobby, but this time I asked to sit in on his checkup since his last one had left him bewildered about both his prognosis and his medications. The visit I witnessed was revealing: the doctor, avoiding eye contact with Dad, talked to Dad's chart while making notes and mumbling conclusions. I suddenly understood Dad's inability to comprehend his condition.

Dad's difficulties with orientation and communication resurfaced when my brothers gifted him with a fax machine for instantaneously sending letters long distance. Though Dad was thrilled to imagine his letters flying through the air to Oregon and California, he never got the hang of manipulating the keys successfully without supervision. The machine was technologically too complicated for him.

Automated phone response systems proved to be equally frustrating. One afternoon I walked in on Dad as he slammed the phone down, grumbling, "I can't get a word in edgewise." Lapsing into a high falsetto, he mimicked the person to whom he thought he had been speaking, "We're sorry, your call cannot be completed as . . . yap, yap, yap." Dad had no idea he'd been trying to converse with a recording—an observation that helped me understand his cynicism about similar encounters with the phone company and his home insurer.

In our early days of caregiving, John and I were stymied when the systems we had expected to physically and emotionally support our parents failed in their stated mission, especially those from top-notch businesses or agencies. Their seemingly inexcusable complexities, compounded by our parents' frequent problems manipulating modern technology, left us wondering how our parents were ever going to continue managing their lives—or for that matter, how we were.

Had we learned earlier about more easily accomplished solutions such as phone amplification, security phone devices, alarm systems, and extended-range antennae for cars, we might have spared ourselves and our parents a lot of frustration. As it was, we ended up demonstrating ways to navigate overly complicated and dehumanizing systems to no avail while witnessing our once-competent parents falter.

If you notice a provider or business being inattentive to the needs of your parent . . .

The inability of adult children to fully comprehend challenges modern systems and technologies may pose to an aging parent is often rooted in a wish to deny the extent of their parent's disabilities, though other contributing factors include the generation gap spanning technological advances, inexperience in empathizing with a parent's circumstances, and a lack of information about possible solutions to problems. By acknowledging the difficulties and exploring a variety of caregiving solutions, you will be able to make better decisions on your parent's behalf.

While inventorying your parent's benefits and hindrances in terms of service providers and technological devices, consider these questions:

- Are you aware of any incapacities that may make it difficult for your parent to comprehend service providers?

- Have you discussed with your parent any communication problems they are having with service providers or advisers?

- Do you give clear feedback to providers or business personnel about improvements needed in senior services? Have you encouraged your parent to do the same?

- Have you explored assistive devices or services, such as phones with large digital dialing pads, extra-loud ringers, or amplifiers; car alarms; or people trained in 'senior tutoring'?

- Do you know whether your parent's assistive supports are helping rather than hindering?

——— COMING OF AGE PASSAGE ———
Admitting your parent's decline

Baptism by Gunfire

When you entertain notions of outwitting your parent, you could be in for a rude awakening.

As parents age, it often becomes increasingly worrisome that they might become suicidal and use objects or medications at hand to inflict self-injury. For us, it was hard not to register the potential danger of Dad's gun because he had posted a sign on his front door announcing, "This house is loaded with a .38-caliber revolver and a mean SOB who knows how to use it." Dad believed this strategy was the best means of protection in a neighborhood that had deteriorated into a high-crime zone.

Although the gun was stored in a coffee table drawer while other weapons were within reach—a billy club in the front hall, a kitchen knife stuffed between Dad's mattress and box springs, and a bottle of Tabasco sauce he could throw into the eyes of an assailant—it was his gun we feared most. Dad's recurring bouts of hopelessness had John and I convinced he just might use it on himself, a concern intensified by our recollection of my great-grandfather, who at age ninety-nine had muttered, "I gotta get out of here or I'll go on forever," stalked into the chicken coop, and shot himself in the head.

So we decided to filch Dad's pawn-shop revolver from the drawer, take it home to empty its bullets, and clandestinely return it unloaded, wagering his glaucoma would keep him unaware of our actions. As I distracted Dad over a plate of Fig Newtons one evening, John removed the pistol and wrapped it in an opaque plastic bag. Immediately we announced our departure, cocking our ears lest Dad's farewell reveal any suspicion. Once home, John stored the gun in the basement, vowing to empty the ammunition in the morning. Knowing Dad's impulses would not get the better of him during the night, we slept well.

As dawn broke the next morning, I ambled home from a brisk stride through our neighborhood. Glancing through our front window, I spotted John in a shaft of sunlight, vacuuming. "Honey, thank you so much!" I hollered, stepping inside.

Over the roar of the machine, he answered, "Well, there's more to this story than goodwill housekeeping." He cut the vacuum's power and announced, "I was trying to get the bullets out of that gun of his, and all of a sudden it went off." Seeing the horror on my face, he added, "It's okay," and directed my gaze to a hole in the ceiling.

Feeling lucky that the bullet had not hit John or our seventy-five-year-old chandelier, we burst into laughter punctuated by an occasional "Oh my God." So intent had we been on sneaking the loaded gun off Dad's premises that we had given no thought to unloading it on ours and, in fact, did not even know how to remove bullets from such a model. With great relief we restored the emptied gun safely to Dad's coffee table and knew that our rude awakening had indeed been another lesson in eldercare.

If you think your parent might inflict self-injury . . .

Like a parent dealing with a child, you may begin designing elaborate schemes–anything to prevent accidents from happening. But such fear-based behaviors can sometimes cause harm in other ways, both physically and emotionally.

To make an inoffensive game plan for possible emergency situations, consider the following questions:

- How would you handle a perceived emergency regarding a parent? Before acting, would you consult reliable sources about your intentions?

- Has your parent experienced depression, or does your parent have suicidal thoughts? Can you convince your parent to get help from a mental health professional?

- Do you feel comfortable going behind your parent's back if they are considering taking their life?

- Do you need to expand your knowledge about firearms, medications, or other means of causing self-injury?

———— COMING OF AGE PASSAGE ————
Realizing that you, like your parents, are a limited edition

The Doctor Is In

Though self-diagnosis has its place, an aging parent who self-medicates can compromise their health.

As our parents became more frail, they increasingly took on the role of diagnostician and designer of treatment for whatever ailed them. To keep them relatively unscathed we had to learn to recognize the gorillas of self-care in their midst.

Finding my dad in the backyard one day, we noticed the rag bandage around his arm smelling of turpentine. "Painting today, Dad?" I asked.

"Nope," he replied. "Been trimming limbs from that maple tree before they completely block the sunlight from a patch of grass. Cut myself up a little with my handsaw, but I've doused my arm in turpentine to keep out the infection." Three days later, his temperature soaring, we took him to the doctor.

At another point, cancerous lesions began decorating Ray's forehead. Like a child with chicken pox, Ray found it impossible to keep from picking the sores. Contrary to his belief that scratching would allow the lesions to scab over and go away, it made them larger. Later, we visited his doctor, who short-circuited their growth with nitrogen.

Impie, for her part, once neglected a wound. Because she had been a nurse, we imagined when she developed a sore on her heel that she would change the dressing daily, but three days later John caught a glimpse of a grimy bandage under her long skirt. We reminded her of the guideline she had shared with patients over the decades: If you can't see or reach your feet and one of them hurts, go to a podiatrist. She coined this motto when a man with diabetes, unaware of his infection, was admitted to her unit and she unraveled his homemade bandage to find one of his toes loose in the dressing. Consequently, we went to a podiatrist and fortunately discovered that Impie only needed to be treated for an infection.

Mom's way of treating infection was to ignore dosage requirements. To save money, she would take prescribed pills every other day until she sensed improvement, stashing the leftovers in the medicine cabinet. She couldn't fathom that the partial therapy had established only a first line of resistance and if infection returned she would have to start the full course all over again.

To our surprise, our parents had also tried alternative therapies. Intermingled with the assorted vitamins they usually took were plastic bottles of zinc, saw palmetto, Saint-John's-wort, and high-fiber capsules. How progressive, we thought, but on interviewing our parents about their reasons for indulging in complementary regimens, as well as their dosages and frequencies, we found their convoluted answers devoid of knowledge concerning these treatments.

It was less surprising to find that convenience figured prominently in our parents' self-styled medical forays. Ray, tired of losing his prescription eyeglasses and having exhausted his health insurance benefits, ordered several pairs by mail. Though the strength of the lenses that arrived failed to compensate for his farsightedness, he concluded it was too bothersome to recover his money and asked to be left alone to "make do" with his purchases.

Likewise my dad, after losing a lot of weight, began having trouble with his false teeth. Taking things literally into his own hands, he attempted to reshape his dentures with a pocketknife. As a result, his teeth not only didn't fit but they hurt. Together we visited a denturist, who recommended a new set of teeth, but when Dad was informed of the cost he hopped off the exam room recliner and stomped out the door. We pureed his food for the rest of his life, except for soft fare like chocolates.

When it comes to ailments considered too personal for discussion, rather than consult a doctor elders frequently resort to over-the-counter medications, sometimes becoming addicted. For example, to help move their bowels women will often ingest a common laxative until they are pooping too much. As an antidote, they may use a nonprescription antidiarrheal, only to become constipated again. Enter enemas—upon which they can become dependent, or worse, addicted.

Similarly, most men don't like to discuss their prostate or incontinence, or admit their stream isn't as strong as it used to be or that to urinate they have to sit on the toilet. Uncomfortable addressing these maladies and assuming they cannot afford medications to alleviate them, many aging men begin wearing pads, electing to live with the situation.

Had John and I gone through our parents' medicine cabinets sooner, we might have better monitored their safety, allaying some of the fallout from self-doctoring by encouraging them to seek proper medical care. Though most such cabinets are generally messy, theirs were scary. Upon close inspection, we discovered topical ointments with expiration dates long past, assorted Band-Aids too old to adhere, jars of powders and pastes with contents unmarked, and myriad prescription bottles containing assorted pills and capsules.

Unfortunately, our parents' motivations for taking things into their own hands appeared contradictory and sometimes dangerous, reflecting an irony that eluded them. Whereas earlier they had staked their lives on the opinions of medical practitioners, now with their well-being perhaps more in jeopardy they were refusing doctors' treatments in favor of their own spurious expertise.

If your parent has assumed erroneous authority for their health care . . .

Falls, bumps, aches and pains, and mysterious symptoms accelerate with aging. But making a doctor's appointment, arranging transportation if necessary, or picking up a prescription can be complicated and stress provoking. Add a pound of need for independence, a few ounces of fear about the unknown such as expenses for office calls or procedures, and the inconvenience of following up, and you've got the ingredients for parental denial, avoidance, or mismanagement of potentially serious health concerns.

Ironically, elders today are asked to take more responsibility for their health, to "partner" with their physicians by becoming informed consumers, and to ensure their end-of-life wishes have been recorded. However, since these requests cannot be fulfilled if common sense should escape your parent's decision making, prepare to take charge. First, let your parent know of your concern for their well-being and about the dangers of self-care. Second, invest in a fresh supply of first-aid provisions, discarding those no longer effective, and make sure your parent has connections with medical professionals for back-up care. If you have noticed an array of prescription bottles, show your parent how to locate expiration dates and review the theory of utilizing a full prescription.

When you suspect there is more to the physical or mental health picture than your parent is presenting, make inquiries and listen closely for clues to set the stage for dialogue. For more perspective on self-diagnosis, consider the following questions:

• What is your parent's attitude about seeking medical help? What influences their perceptions about this kind of assistance?

• Have you and your parent discussed the scope of injuries, illnesses, and medical emergencies that can be triggered by aging? Have you assessed the currency and condition of your parent's medical supplies and equipment? Have you posted important phone numbers in case of emergencies?

• If you have concerns regarding your parent's judgment about getting medical help, have you shared them? Can you and your parent agree on situations in which medical support is needed?

——— COMING OF AGE PASSAGE ———
Refusing to be gullible

Deck the Halls of the Emergency Room

If a parent has a medical crisis during the holidays, family traditions can easily become less sacrosanct.

One year we thought our Christmas was going to be especially peaceful since our two adult children would be feasting at their respective in-laws' homes and we were set to have a quiet dinner with my father. Before fetching him, I put a roast in the oven, turned on some soothing music, and stacked logs for a fire, while John dropped in on his mother.

When I arrived at Dad's house, he was shivering on the front porch, grousing, "Thought you'd never get here. You're five minutes late."

"Well, I'm here now, Pop. Merry Christmas," I said, planting a loud kiss on his forehead.

We cruised across town under a navy sky, wondering if it would snow. As we stopped for a train, Dad took advantage of the moment to ask, "What do you think of these?" Hiking his pants to mid-calf level, he exposed legs twice their normal size and oozing from the inflammation.

"Dad, you're *leaking!*" I exclaimed. "Are you in pain?"

"Nope. Pants are just a little tight around the cuffs, and I couldn't get my socks on so I cut them down like your mom's footies. These legs are really swollen, aren't they?"

Worried, I fired off a message to his doctor from my cell phone. Then I called John and asked him to meet us at home as soon as possible.

Soon after we had all piled into the living room, the doctor phoned, suggesting we take Dad to the nearest emergency room to determine the cause for his edema and asking if Dad was taking his meds. "Yep, every day," Dad told me. Before heading out, I set the timer on the stove so it could baby-sit the roast in our absence.

At the ER, we were sequestered in a curtained stall where, despite the season to be jolly, we witnessed a medical chamber of horrors. The man in the stall next to us had been badly burned by an exploding camp stove. Across the way was a young girl, her forearm hanging at a right angle from a plunge she had taken into a snowbank. And beyond were more casualties: someone pleading for a fix, a toddler trying to cough up the glass holiday ornament he had swallowed, and a woman who had unsuccessfully induced labor after taking bets on birthing the town's first Christmas baby.

Two hours after our arrival, the attending physician began interrogating Dad, who responded as dishonestly as possible, assuring the doctor he'd been taking his meds, felt great, and had no clue what all the fuss was about. I thought, *Not only is my dad a chronic liar, he is unwilling to take responsibility for his condition. Worse, the doctor is nodding his head in apparent agreement.*

As the questioning continued, I took advantage of Dad's hearing impairment and began whispering negations to his fibs, but the physician paid no attention to me. Panicky, I approached an attendant, who informed me that if I considered my dad's replies incorrect, I should not take issue with him but rather ask a nurse to act as my intermediary with the doctor.

Six hours later, Dad, John, and I exited the ER with new meds, though we still had to phone in Dad's insurance subscriber number since he'd forgotten to bring along his ID card. By now, the roast posed a health risk and the carols on the CD player seemed too ironic a contrast to the day, but Dad nevertheless announced he was ready for a hearty holiday feast.

"How would you like a greasy burger and a sinful chocolate malt instead?" I offered, forgetting that few fast-food joints were open on Christmas Day. He looked disappointed but agreed.

At 4:00 p.m., we found one open restaurant. Unfortunately its milkshake machine was on the fritz.

No sooner did we reach Dad's door than he dashed inside for a good stiff drink. As for John and I, back home at last we tossed the roast, excavated the freezer, nuked a container of archived tomato-basil soup, and mused that mincemeat pie would be superb for breakfast.

In retrospect, we realized we were unprepared for this entire series of events because we had never imagined a parent needing to go to the ER. We should have maintained a list of Dad's medications, including names, potencies, and dosages. We should have kept his healthcare subscriber's ID on hand, too. Additionally, it would have been desirable to bring along his durable power of attorney documents for the hospital records. We now recognize as well that the role of the ER staff is to help patients move efficiently through the maze of healthcare services, a function that includes, when necessary, the eliciting of honest communication.

If you need to take your parent to the emergency room . . .

Accompanying a parent to the emergency room is an emotionally unsettling experience. To be better prepared, first realize that imagining a parent will never need ER services is analogous to living under the illusion they are never going to die. A visit to the ER is highly likely and apt to go most smoothly if you bring along medications, information about your parent's condition, and possibly an advance directive or durable power of attorney document. In the event that your parent is unable to provide accurate input or ask questions, assistance may be needed.

After leaving the ER, make sure that any prescription your parent received there does not duplicate a medication they are already taking. Also ensure it won't combine dangerously with other pharmaceuticals or over-the-counter therapies they are on. If you have any questions, contact your parent's physician.

To prepare in advance for an ER visit with an aging parent, consider the following questions:

- Have you consulted your parent's physician about the advisability of going to the ER as opposed to an urgent or immediate care center?

- Are you familiar with the Medicare or health insurance benefits available to your parent?

- Do you know where your parent's most current medication and legal records are stored? Do you have copies in case they are misplaced or lost?

- Is your parent able to assume responsibility for taking medications? Do you understand the side effects of your parent's medications taken singly or in combination with other pharmaceuticals?

- If your parent might fail to provide the ER doctor with correct information, have you sought ways to clarify any misconceptions?

——— COMING OF AGE PASSAGE ———

Realizing life throws you curves despite what you do

PART 2 ————

Hanging On

Acceptance of a parent's need for ongoing assistance can dawn slowly, often after years of denial. The tendency is to seek various means for continuing life as it was yet simultaneously provide parents with support, eventually realizing these paths are contradictory.

Such realizations are usually hard won. At first you may act out of crisis, keeping desperation at bay by settling for the quickest, least expensive, and most convenient solutions, such as finding a neighbor to check on your parent every so often—until they resign out of exhaustion. Persevering with coping mechanisms, you may then begin rationalizing, having tantrums, zoning out, or distorting, saying such things as "It seems Mom can't remember squat, so why don't we take turns calling her on our work breaks to see if she's okay," or "Look, anyone who can get a perfect score on his first driver's test can't be that bad a driver. Let's just ask Dad to stay off the freeway." Then there's Let's Make a Deal: "Okay, God. If we do weekend duty with Mom, will you make sure her money holds out?"

But despite such strategies, the lives of once competent parents continue raging out of control. Fearing that your short stint in eldercare could turn into a marathon, you may start losing things like sleep, a social life, and predictability.

In our case, over a matter of months John and I were catapult-ed from awareness of our parents' aging into the greater realities of eldercare. Suddenly we were participants in systems we knew little about—managed care, hospitals, and long-term provisions. Though our parents were granted membership privileges such as the Patient's Bill of Rights, as their overseers we felt bereft of the knowl-edge and experience needed to guide them. After years of being effective parents and professionals, we were now neophytes ques-tioning our every move, unsure about hiring relief caregivers, mak-ing end-of-life decisions, and even becoming unavailable to our parents by phone over the dinner hour.

For most adult children facing eldercare, the learning curve at this point grows rapidly, as does a spectrum of unexpected feelings. You might experience a strong need for control, or begin resenting your parent for no longer acting like a parent or for turning your world upside down overnight. If you live far away, you might be riddled with anxiety and guilt.

Your parent, meanwhile, may fight every change you propose, hammering you head-on with evidence of their prowess or with manipulation if they don't get the results they desire. Your parent's most ardent crusades, perhaps focused on abilities (like driving) or well-being (especially vision and digestion), are apt to be motivat-ed primarily by a need for independence and preservation of dig-nity. Yet in the face of all these challenges, committing to eldercare with a vow to hang on can enhance your awareness of the rewards that await you.

Hiding Behind the Answering Machine

When your parent has dementia, feelings of overwhelm can lead to short-term solutions that may come back to haunt you.

In the early days of safekeeping John's mother Impie, we attempted to batten down the hatches by arranging for check-in support every couple of hours. That way John and I could breathe deeply over supper, confident that she would be fine until his arrival shortly after 6:00 p.m. to make certain she had eaten, chat with her, and tuck her into bed.

Then the phone calls started. Impie began by leaving messages on our answering machine while we were at work; but she had enough moxie to then realize that if she waited until after 5:00 p.m., a live person would answer, proffering help and attention. Initially on reaching us she had a simple question or two that we could answer reassuringly enough for her to hang up. But as time passed, her calls were more frequent, eventually taxing our patience.

The nightly ritual had become one of the only predictable aspects of our lives. The first call would go something like this: "I can't find my toenail clippers. Do you know where they are?"

"No, Mom. We haven't seen them. Did you look in the medicine cabinet?"

During the second call she might say, "I can't find my toenail clippers. Did you do something with them?"

"No, as I mentioned earlier, we haven't seen them. How about looking in your purse."

Calling a third time, she would remark, "This is very important. What did you do with my clippers? I need them right now."

"I know, Mom. Why don't you wait till I'm there this evening and I'll help you look."

No matter how often we told her she was calling repeatedly

with the same question, she persevered in her quest. After several evenings of multiple calls between 5:00 and 6:00 p.m., we finally resorted to letting the answering machine pick up messages so we could eat. One evening we counted fifteen dinner-hour calls from Impie, her anxiety escalating with each one. After the first six or seven calls, there was irritation in her voice as she said, "Oh, hell, they aren't going to answer," then "Hello. Hello? *Hello!*" after which she slammed down the receiver. In her final pitch she declared, "This is Impie Goeller, I-M-P-I-E G-O-E-L-L-E-R, and I want you to call me right now at 664-0119," which was not her phone number but ours.

One call made us realize Impie had no recollection of recent events. The phone rang just as we were about to dive into a tuna salad. We rolled our eyes, assuming the caller was Impie, but instead it was one of her neighbors advising us that he'd spotted her wandering in front of his house. Unable to reach us by phone, she had apparently decided to find us on foot. We needed another strategy to preserve dinnertime sanctity, but first we had to navigate our way out of the labyrinth we had created.

Trying to absorb the reality of Impie's weakening mind, John and I struggled with the notion of Alzheimer's, a disease we had little knowledge of. Though we understood the malady hung from the mobile of dementia, it was difficult to integrate the fact that there would be no clear-cut diagnosis and that without a medical breakthrough her disease would persist for the rest of her life.

We preferred to do battle with Impie's symptoms: to furnish her with more reminders, count on her logic to kick in, and trust blindly that she had the wherewithal to remember to turn off her hot plate and keep the doors locked. However, like her repeated attempts to reach us by phone, our endeavors to have her act more logically and responsibly bore no fruit. Consequently we had to face the terrible truth about Impie's condition and learn how to deal with Alzheimer's in the context of our commitment to care for her.

If you haven't accepted the fact that your parent's behavior is likely to get worse instead of better . . .

If you haven't made the emotional transition necessary to fully comprehend your aging parent's declining physical or mental health, be assertive about your boundaries and yet fiercely dedicated to honesty. It may be necessary to begin gathering more diagnostic information from professionals, or to research various support options. To help bridge the gap between what was and what is as you bear witness to your parent's deterioration, consider the following questions:

- Have you been rationalizing your parent's unusual behavior or minimizing its significance, seeing only aspects of your parent's competence? On the other hand, have you been exaggerating danger signs?

- What do you understand about your parent's diagnosis? Where can you access more information?

- Are you aware of emotions surfacing as you learn more about your parent's condition? How might you process them?

——— COMING OF AGE PASSAGE ———

Hanging on to boundaries under duress

Throw Mama on the Plane

Thinking you can do everything yourself, it's easy to end up clutching at straws in a desperate search for solutions.

After the first six months of daily check-ins with his mother Impie, John suffered a major meltdown. He had disregarded the warning signs of burnout—increased irritability, difficulty sleeping, and twinges of depression—until one day he could no longer count on the sunrise to lighten his self-appointed solo mission. Feeling trapped and frantic, he called his older brother seven states away to see about taking Impie in for a couple of weeks.

Although his brother agreed, the plan was easier conceived than executed. First John had to find an affordable, safe way to get a hazy senior citizen suffering from Alzheimer's across the country. Then, after booking a flight requiring her to change planes in Denver, he needed to facilitate the transfer. As if that were not enough, on their way to the airport Impie had a lucid moment, asking pointedly, "Hey, do you think I should really be traveling by myself?" Closing his eyes, John managed an "I don't know," said a prayer, and drove on, more eager than ever for his two weeks of liberation.

At the check-in counter, John's concern deepened because Impie, looking puzzled, had begun wringing her hands and reading the overhead banners aloud, over and over. Suddenly he was approached by an acquaintance, who as it turned out was booked on the same flight as Impie and delighted at the prospect of seeing her to her destination. John nearly wept with gratitude.

Six hours later he arrived home from work to two phone messages, the first confirming his mother's safe arrival and the second, from the airline, alerting him that Impie had been rescheduled for a nonstop return trip. That evening John reflected, "You know, once you ask for help it really can show up—though not in the forms you expect."

If you might be verging on caregiver burnout . . .

Most family caregivers have difficulty asking for help because they envision themselves capable of dealing with the responsibilities single-handedly. Unfortunately, in such instances it can take a crisis to discover that healthy caregiving entails reaching out for support.

If, while caring for your parent, you are out of control, anxious, overly emotional, depressed, compulsive, or dependent on drugs or alcohol, take a break. Perhaps enlist the services of a counselor or join a caregiver's support group to regain a healthy grip on life. Sooner is better than later, for many caregivers become ill, or die before their charges. A short break daily or at least weekly may suffice, boosting not only your health but also the welfare of your parent.

It is important to remember that caregiver burnout also affects elders. This finding alone can help you overcome embarrassment about arranging regular time-outs for your own well-being. To prepare in advance for good self-care practices, consider the following questions:

- How are you really doing, and on what criteria do you base this evaluation? Can you self-monitor or do you require feedback from trusted others?

- How difficult is it for you to ask for assistance? How willing are you to expand your outreach?

- Do you procrastinate, or wait for a crisis before initiating desirable changes? How might you break these habits?

——— COMING OF AGE PASSAGE ———
Learning it is not shameful to ask for help

Bypassing the Bypass

When one parent has an emergency, the other may prioritize their own needs over those of their children, forcing you to adjust your expectations.

On a damp Saturday afternoon my distressed mother called to say, "Honey, your dad has had some heart trouble. I took him to the hospital." My alarm system blared as I pitched questions: "How bad is it?" "When did it happen?" Discovering that eighteen hours had elapsed since the attack, I overrode my impulse to scream and instead croaked, "Mom, why didn't you call?"

"I just didn't," she replied, hanging up.

Moments later I arrived at the intensive care unit. Tremors ricocheted through every cell of my body as I demanded to see my father. Finally, a nurse led me to the cubicle where Dad was lying. He looked awful, but the prognosis was good following the quadruple bypass he had undergone.

When Dad inquired about Mom, I changed the subject, asking him to tell me what had happened. He recalled climbing a ladder to flush pine needles out of a rain gutter, feeling a pain in his chest, dismounting, alerting Mom, and surviving a ragged ride to the nearest ER. Inaudibly I murmured, "We were lucky this time!"

A week after Dad was transferred to a private room, a discharge planner appeared in the doorway to discuss the necessary measures for Dad's return home. As Mom and I started a list of contacts for support, my rage surfaced. I demanded, "Why didn't you call right away when you admitted Dad to the hospital? What if he had died and I hadn't been able to say good-bye? He's your husband–but he's also my dad!"

My mother stroked her thighs, her eyes and mouth pulling into pencil lines. Eventually she replied, "I just couldn't deal with you too. I needed to come home and howl and throw things and curse

God. I have the right to some space before the rest of the world comes crashing in." The image of my gentle mother yelling at God and heaving objects adjusted my kaleidoscope from anger to tenderness.

Afterward I pondered the dilemma of who should know and when, arriving at the insight that when the time comes for my parents to leave, it probably will be too late to say good-bye. Ever since, no matter how often I expressed my love to them, or walked away mad, made amends, and opened my heart again, I still caught myself waiting at the Crossroads of Remorse, muttering, "If only I'd told them one more time." Reflecting on the crisis now, I realize that because my mother had always been sensitive to my needs I was jolted by her behavior after Dad's heart attack. However, not only did I get a crash course in broadening my perspective of Mom, I also learned to temper my self-centeredness and acknowledge Mom's right to act in keeping with her needs.

If your parent has difficulty communicating about life-threatening issues . . .

Coming to terms with dissimilar communication styles is a life-long challenge, particularly when a parent views self-reliance as the cornerstone of their identity. Asking for open communication in such instances can present a setup for frustration.

If at the time of a family crisis you begin unconsciously competing with your parent for center stage, the first step in overcoming this impulse is to realize that everyone will be at their worst until the storm passes. The second step is to recognize that life with elderly parents is fraught with crises and that saner responses come from assessing not only your own needs but those of other family members. To broaden your perspective on the needs of various family members during a crisis, explore the following questions:

- Are you able to see your parent as a vulnerable individual facing difficulties that are distinct from yours?

- Are you committed to resolving parental crises by bridging communication gaps and clarifying expectations for the future?

- If robbed of the opportunity to say good-bye or gain closure with a dying parent, how would you feel? What can you do now to prevent this from happening?

———— COMING OF AGE PASSAGE ————
Respecting your place in the pecking order

The Impermanent Permanent

Securing occasional respite care seems imperative in times of desperation, but crisis strategies can end up substituting one problem for another.

When our children were young, our parents delighted in caring for them at a moment's notice. Endeavoring to level the playing field, I gave my parents coupons for food preparation and house maintenance services, and John ran errands for his dad, while I cut and permed his mother's hair whenever she desired.

Impie and I progressed with the times, chucking the old curling rods in favor of swank rollers, and experimenting with brands of waving lotion until finding one capable of wreaking little havoc on our nostrils. I sighed in relief each time she approved of her "do," which generally occurred about two hours after we'd begun. But when Ray died and Impie wandered more deeply into the jungle of

Alzheimer's disease, perming her hair became a four-hour ordeal.

One night after I complained, John remarked, "Hey, I just heard the cosmetology department at the community college is looking for volunteers the students can practice on. Why don't we try *them* next time?" Thrilled at the prospect of having the time to ourselves, I agreed. John scheduled an appointment for Impie the following Wednesday, and we arranged for an outing of our own.

After John escorted her to the college, he returned to pick me up, saying, "I explained she has Alzheimer's and is sometimes erratic, but if spoken to quietly she would follow directions. There were four students, and they all assured me they knew how to handle her. Figuring nothing catastrophic would happen, I scampered out before they could change their minds."

John and I, savoring a leisurely lunch and matinee, had no trouble escaping into our long-lost normalcy. Unfortunately, it came abruptly to an end when we returned to find all four interns huddling in a corner of the salon as eighty-two-year-old Impie, holding court with a cane, shouted, "Look what they did to me!"

Striving for an Afro effect, the interns had brushed her kinks into a coif that, extending at least three inches from her scalp, made her head look like a giant dandelion gone to seed. John paid the seven-dollar fee, left a twenty-dollar tip, and taking Impie by the elbow, steered her toward the car vowing never again to darken the door of this place.

Later, we all agreed on the virtues of straight hair cropped short, a style that took only half an hour to maintain. We even contracted with a mobile salon service to come tend to Impie's hair when I wasn't available. But sadly, within a few months the nuances of hairstyles no longer mattered to her because the work crews in her mind had shut down more highways.

In retrospect, John and I realized that in being overly eager for a time-out from caregiving we had tossed common sense to the wind, not only overestimating the students' savvy about working with elders but also minimizing Impie's difficulties in adapting to a new environment. Still in the early stages of our caregiving, we had failed to piece together a viable plan for periodic respite care. Among other things, we had balked at buying a cell phone, considering it just one more piece of technology to maintain, and so provided no way for the students to reach us.

If you are desperately seeking respite care for your parent . . .

Respite care provides assistance to caregivers in need of a break. Respite helpers include volunteers known as Good Samaritans, state-supported agency workers, and employees of private businesses offering in-home services. Some are available on a daytime basis only. Select retirement homes and nursing facilities are equipped to accommodate elders for limited periods of time both day and night.

The search for adequate respite care is well worth the time and effort it takes. If you decide to recruit someone to periodically assist you out of the goodness of their heart, make sure they have both the physical capacity to tend to your parent's needs and a realistic understanding of elders. If you cannot locate a Good Samaritan, review your budget for cuts that would free up reserves for paying hired help. Money spent on short-term eldercare, an expense that allows for your personal revitalization, can prevent or delay the hiring of permanent eldercare.

In the event you need crisis support before doing your homework, call your local Area Agency on Aging for referrals. If your parent lives elsewhere, the Eldercare Locator can connect you with the closest Area Agency on Aging (see page 235). In either instance, explain your situation and request phone numbers of providers who offer respite care on short notice. Then do what you can to find a more suitable arrangement, considering the following questions:

- Are you familiar with respite care options in your community or your parent's?
- Have you developed criteria for selecting a suitable candidate?

• Have you consulted with professionals to determine your parent's capacity for adapting to new locations and unfamiliar people?

———— COMING OF AGE PASSAGE ————
Admitting your limitations

To Tube or Not to Tube, That Is the Question

No matter how thoroughly you and your parent have discussed their end-of-life wishes, you may not feel confident making the final decisions.

One day before dawn, my mother woke up with a fierce pain in her head, attempted to walk, and slammed into a bedroom wall. Unbeknownst to her, she was having a stroke in the left hemisphere of her brain. When I tried communicating with her, she clearly understood what I was saying but her responses were garbled.

At the acute care unit, her family physician was guardedly optimistic. Grimacing, he asked, "Do you want her to have a feeding tube?"

The neurosurgeon chimed in with, "A pressure monitor will tell us about the damage that has occurred. Shall we proceed?"

I remembered my mother's instructions: "No heroic measures if I ever have a stroke." Even so, my heart urged me forward, clinging to a shard of hope that she might survive, go through rehabilitation, and return to a quality life. I nodded, agreeing with the staff that she should get the tube and wear a pressure monitor. Fifty-six days later and marginally improved despite having yanked her feeding tube out seven times, Mom was pummeled by a second stroke.

Wails of lamentation offered up the insight that I had not honored her wishes because I was not ready to let her go. There followed a hangover heavy with self-incrimination. Once aware that this reproach would only make her death worse, I found self-forgiveness.

If you are unsettled about making life-support decisions for a parent who is no longer able to speak for themselves . . .

Even when parents are clear about their wishes, end-of-life circumstances can be colored by ambiguity. Discrepancies in the interpretation of parental desires, lack of information, or medical advisers' statements such as, "Well, if it were my parent . . .," can hurl decision makers into a turmoil. Therefore, it is a good idea to think through possible scenarios ahead of time and arrive at manageable guidelines for making the tough decisions. For example, you could reflect on your parent's value system and how that might suggest direction in the event of a crisis. Or you could discuss hypothetical situations with trusted relatives and gauge their reactions.

Although there are often no easy solutions at the time of crisis, to prepare yourself in advance, contemplate the following questions:

- Has your parent drafted detailed directives concerning potential situations and shared them with you or others?

- If your parent has not delineated life-support preferences, which of their most cherished values can help guide you through these types of decisions?

- Do you have the courage to assert your authority and trust your intuition, regardless of the opinions of medical experts?

———— COMING OF AGE PASSAGE ————
Realizing tough decisions have to be made

Mystery at the Nursing Home

Visiting your parent in a nursing home can be analogous to starring in a whodunit.

As they aged, both my parents stated repeatedly, "Never put me in a nursing home," appeals to which my brothers and I blindly assented. However, after Mom's stroke and subsequent stay in the hospital's intensive care unit, we were advised to find her a nursing home because she needed "heavy care." Despite her past requests, I could see no alternative.

Haunting images from 1950s caroling expeditions to "old folks' homes" filled me with apprehension as John and I began a depressing search for nursing homes. When no beds were available in the better ones, we tiptoed through less desirable facilities, sick at heart at the smell of urine, the gray noise of television, and the chatter of the infirm. Finally, a bed became available in a place given high marks by professionals we knew, whereupon we labored over dozens of forms then selected clothing from home and keepsakes for the room Mom would share with another woman.

After tailing the ambulance from the hospital to her new dwelling, I tried to ignore the fright engraved on Mom's face as she was carried inside. I consoled myself by replacing my negative images of nursing homes with expectations of a positive experience. Surely nurses would come running when Mom needed help; she would connect with kindred souls, bringing the sparkle back to her eyes; the occupational and physical therapy would accelerate her recovery; and she would count among the three-quarters of nursing home occupants who eventually return to their own homes.

Bolstered by these prospects, I was later shocked when Mom's headset was stolen, along with an audiotape containing songs my uncle had sung for her; it resurfaced after we left a note pleading for its return. I was also distressed to discover Mom trapped in an S-position after sliding from the seat of her wheelchair one morning, and perplexed to hear she'd been uncooperative during a therapy session.

The plot thickened one afternoon while I was pushing her wheelchair down the hallway past a male aide who hailed her with, "Hi, Jeannie, how are you doing this morning?" Visibly shaken, she managed to blurt out, "You . . . son . . . of a . . . bitch." Turning to the young man, I asked, "Do you know why she is angry? Did something happen?" His response was a hasty "Oh, you never know what to expect with stroke patients."

Suspicions played hide-and-seek with my mind. Had my mother sustained an accident? Had he hurt her? When I questioned her, with instructions to squeeze my hand once to signal "yes" and twice for "no," she wouldn't cooperate. Nor did conferences with the facility's administration and staff stifle my mounting anxieties. My only option was to resign myself to a series of unsolved mysteries while personally championing Mom's well-being.

If your parent needs nursing home care . . .

If you anticipate placing your parent in a nursing home, learn about your rights and those of your parent. If you are the power of attorney and possess an advance directives document, ask the facility to file copies of it. Should your parent become unable to speak, you as their advocate can then appeal for support and action with the home's administrator or the local state ombudsman to assure your parent's wishes will be respected regardless of the opinions of medical personnel.

In addition, explore how your parent's stay in a nursing home would be funded and understand the differences between Medicare, Medicaid, and other types of coverage. To further prepare for the possibility of taking your parent to a nursing home, see Appendix F, pages 247–249, and also consider the following questions:

- Have you discussed the nursing home option with your parent? If your parent asks not to be put in a nursing home, are you prepared to be realistic, saying, for example, "I can't make that promise, but I can pledge to do my best to ensure you receive the finest care possible"?

- Have you visited several facilities, dropping in without announcing your arrival, asking to see the latest inspection report and complaint records, inquiring about the role of nutrition in overall care, determining if transportation is available to local events and if activities are encouraged, and speaking with residents?

- Are your expectations realistic about your parent's experience in a chosen setting?

- How will your parent's stay be financed beyond Medicare? Do you understand what Medicare does and does not fund? Does your parent qualify for Medicaid? Does your parent have supplemental coverage such as long-term health insurance or a Medigap policy, or will they need to pay privately?

- How can you actively participate in your parent's care? Would you be encouraged to attend care conferences, interact with staff, and speak up when you have concerns?

——— COMING OF AGE PASSAGE ———
Lowering expectations

Late-Life Makeover

Recapturing earlier images of an ailing loved one is an integral part of grieving.

In the weeks following my mother's first stroke, Dad fashioned messages of love and encouragement to tack to the walls and ceiling of her room in the nursing home. No matter how eagerly he called her attention to them, she would turn away. The spectacle was heartbreaking to anyone who happened to be watching.

When the love notes didn't work and Mom wouldn't or couldn't smile, Dad hung a framed Kinko's photo of her from their first year of marriage above his television and, with his faded blue eyes, periodically scanned the outline of her brunette hair, her perfect teeth, the curves of her torso and limbs, saying, "Hey, you're my poster girl. Look at that smile!" Turning to me, he'd add, "Your mom was voted best legs when I was in the legislature." It was this image he preferred to visit instead of the person she was now, and so his time with her gradually waned.

Wondering if Mom was taking his absence personally, I attempted to compensate for Dad's diminished attention by redoubling my efforts to communicate with her. But just after dawn one morning as I sat down the hallway from Mom's room waiting for her to wake up, Dad arrived, apparently on a quest to make Mom better reflect the image of her he fondly recalled. He marched down the corridor so intent on his mission that he did not notice me.

I could hear the nurse's aide speaking to him. "She's been asleep for several hours. Couldn't even get her to occupational therapy yesterday afternoon. Why don't I just leave you two alone for a little bit."

A short time later he exited and, startled to see me, remarked, "She's sleeping. I'll be back later."

I nodded and replied, "I'll give her a quick squeeze and walk out with you."

Entering her room, I immediately noticed that Mom's graying eyebrows were dark brown and her cheeks adorned with magenta circles. Realizing Dad had made her up to resemble how she had looked in her youth, I simultaneously laughed and wept, touched by his memories of her.

Following Dad's makeover of Mom, John and I continued refuting reality by petitioning hope and holding family vigils at Camp No Way. I refused to transfer Mom's favorite clothes, renewed her library card, and began inviting family members home for the next round of holidays ten months later. Looking back, I'm confident Mom's body had told her it was dying and she had fast-forwarded to acceptance, for she seemed to tolerate all of our fussing, as if viewing it from the perspective of an observer rather than a participant.

If you or other family members are resisting saying good-bye to your parent . . .

Today, most people are familiar with the stages of grief, typically progressing from immobilization to denial, anger, bargaining, depression, testing, and finally acceptance. Others are less sequential in their approach. In either case, the time spent in any phase appears to decrease the more the attendant emotions are expressed rather than repressed.

Dad, recovering from shock, braved my mother's nursing-home status with denial and a trace of bargaining, telling himself, *By invoking the younger Jeanne, maybe I can erase this awful turn of events and start over.* If you find yourself knee-deep in denial, waging a war against reality, you can overcome the pain of resistance by allowing your feelings to emerge. Eventually you will recognize anger, a force capable of propelling you through the worst moments of loss and into a world forever changed. To further prepare for your parent's leave-taking, consider the following questions:

- In general, do you find it easier to say hello than good-bye? Are you willing to overcome fears of exploring farewells?

- Are you able to detach from other family members' expressions of denial and yet appreciate their authenticity?

- If you feel the need to grieve, how will you go about this healing work?

- In working through grief, might certain activities be helpful, such as journaling, sharing memories with your parent or other loved ones, reading about people who confronted death, or joining a support group?

———— COMING OF AGE PASSAGE ————
Saying good-bye so you can say hello

"What Do You Mean You're Kicking Her Out?"

Restrictions imposed by housing facilities sometimes appear in the contract; at other times, you'll learn about them only if your parent is asked to leave.

As an ice storm curled its fingers around our small community, robbing it of heat and electricity, John and I gathered firewood, bought candles, and renewed our bonds with neighbors. But our spirit of adventure soon gave way to domestic tension.

The caregivers for John's mother Impie and Aunt Lyna, who resided together in the Goeller family home seven miles away, could not keep the fires burning round the clock, let alone manage the stress. By day six, their pleas were relentless—for more kindling, someone to listen, a mediator to help settle quarrels between the sisters.

The dispute started because Impie had snatched Lyna's false teeth, cramming them into her mouth before Lyna could cross the room in her wheelchair. When John arrived, Lyna snarled, "Your mother is wearing my teeth!" True to form, Impie denied the charge.

"Well, to whom do *those* dentures belong?" he queried, pointing at Lyna's mouth.

"They're your mother's," she replied. "What else could I use when I couldn't get mine?"

We decided to relocate the sisters while waiting out the storm, so John began a search for temporary housing. It turned out a small group home with restored power had space for both women on a short-term basis—if they would consent to sleeping in the foyer. Greatly relieved and willing to consider a heated chicken coop at that point, John delivered Impie and Lyna to the respite facility, dashing back soon afterward to fetch their medications, forgotten in the rush.

When he returned to the facility fifteen minutes later, the owner met him at the doorway snorting between hyperventilations. "Your mother can stay, but I won't have that other woman in this house," she gasped. "No one with a mouth like that will be allowed under my roof."

Beyond the proprietor's silhouette, John spotted his aunt smirking. "What do you mean you're kicking her out?" he asked.

Lyna squealed, "Get me the hell out of here! She may be a registered nurse, but she doesn't know a whit about transferring people from wheelchairs. I was in so much pain when she hoisted me into bed that I darn near fainted. Is there room for one more at your place?"

We had managed to keep warm during the storm by huddling together under a down quilt, and though the image of squeezing Lyna between us held the promise of added body heat, John shuddered at the thought. He briefly considered taking her to an all-night restaurant, harnessing her to a padded chair, and dropping by occasionally to join her for a cup of tea, but realized he couldn't continue to function without sleep. Reaching for his cell phone, he called a cousin 180 miles away in Missoula, Montana, leaving a request on the answering machine: could they take Lyna for a couple of days while he inquired about temporary housing for her?

During John's drive home with Lyna in tow, power was returned to the community. He was grateful to have wriggled through another tight spot. But invented emergencies flashed across the radar screen in his head, and he worried what would happen if Lyna eventually filled our life's container to the brim, overwhelming us.

Upon further reflection, we realized we were entrenched in a pattern of reacting to emergencies rather than anticipating them and that we'd become accustomed to crisis mode—retrieving missing items, coordinating trips to the ER, picking up medications, finding substitute caregivers. It made sense that since relocation had never been among our drills, tension was higher than usual during this incident.

If your loved one suddenly needs emergency housing . . .

No matter how hard you work to create a secure environment for your parent, a natural disaster, accident, or their sudden deterioration might force you into an immediate search for alternative housing. Backup options are essential even if your parent is in a retirement community, assisted living unit, or nursing home, because although the fine print of your contract may state that the facility will arrange for temporary housing, there is no way to know in advance how well your parent will adapt. Some elders adjust well to such disruptions, while others get scared and confused.

If emergency housing becomes an issue, you may need to make a quick judgment call, taking into account your parent's personality, physical and emotional needs, and past relocation history. Consequently, it is a good idea to prepare in advance, researching several facilities and clarifying your parent's needs. In anticipation of the need for a sudden move, consider the following questions:

- Do you have a backup plan for emergency housing? If not, do you know how to preview short-term care facilities?

- What is the best way to support your parent emotionally during a sudden change in housing?

- Are you prepared to advise emergency housing personnel about circumstances that might trigger unpleasant reactions in your parent, as well as other difficult behaviors likely to surface?

——— COMING OF AGE PASSAGE ———
Learning multiple crisis management

Neighborhood Parent Watch

If your parent becomes the neighborhood tyrant, chasms can erupt in your caregiver support system.

One by one, the neighbors became alienated by my dad's verbal assaults. Quick to express injustices he felt he had sustained, Dad rationalized each incident with a mixture of profanity and righteous indignation. Offenders included a divorcée who had emptied her car ashtray onto the pavement in front of his home, a dog that had done its daily dump on his parking strip, and a rapper who had disrupted his sleep by booming a CD just yards from his bedroom window. I concluded: his frustrations are legitimate, but his responses inappropriate.

Then my mother died. Grieving his loss, Dad stopped answering the phone, so I canvassed the neighborhood in search of someone willing to keep a watchful eye on him. Yvonne, who had arrived from Czechoslovakia in the 1940s, was kind enough to offer and unwittingly became Dad's next victim. Mom had always been able to decipher Yvonne's thick accent, but Dad evidently could not. One day she approached him to discuss a community zoning issue of mutual interest, and he exploded, yelling, "Yvonne, you've been in the country for five decades and I still can't figure out a damn thing you're saying! Why don't you go back to Czechoslovakia, where they can understand you?" Stunned, the woman scuttled off to safety.

Later in the day when I heard he had attacked a good person and lacked remorse, I asked, "If Mom had been here, how would she handle this situation?"

"She probably would have stopped me," he replied. Mom protected the world from Dad and Dad from the world, I realized. Without her, he had become a loose cannon blasting with inconsolable grief.

The next day when I visited he snapped, "Well, hell. Jeanne's not here to apologize to Yvonne. So I went down and told her I was sorry, that I'm just a grumpy old man. We had a good talk. You know, she's been widowed twice now." His voice broke as he noted that Yvonne's forty-three-year-old daughter was still at the family home, paralyzed with muscular dystrophy. He then recalled the thousands of afternoons he had returned home from a job he never liked and, passing Yvonne's garden, felt uplifted by the child's movements amidst a vibrant array of color. He had called her Maria of the Daylilies, an angel-child catching him with her radiant beam.

Now, he momentarily forgot his loneliness, yet his anger had hurled me back to my childhood. I caught glimpses of my dad frozen in rage and each family member's response to it, including my own obsession with perfectionism. Whenever he complained about my mother's lackadaisical attitude toward housework, I would unobtrusively dust and pick up the clutter. When he was displeased with my penmanship, I'd practice ovals late into the night. His flare-ups over my more core shortcomings had been immobilizing. Attempting to alleviate his pain and avoid mine, I assumed variations of these behaviors in my adult life, although over time I became less reactive and more self-directed. I returned from this brief retrospective with a more expanded view of my father as a man once inspired by the sight of a child in a garden.

If your parent's behavior seems out of control . . .

The fury of an aging parent is apt to create chasms in your support system and also awaken a painful realization of the extent to which your family was organized around this parent's control. Each outburst of parental frustration may prompt you to follow bread crumbs back to your childhood to reflect on family dynamics. Though these memories may at first provoke anxiety, ultimately they can enhance self-knowledge and family healing.

Further, increased contact with a parent who expresses anger can expand your limited vision of them. Once you see beyond the curmudgeon's costume, you might appreciate the broader range of their behavior, catching a glimmer of their rainbow before it is too late.

To prepare for dealing with a difficult aging parent, consider the following questions:

- If you have shared your concerns about difficult behavior with your parent and nothing changed, what other action can you take?
- Have you consulted professionals or others who know your parent well, to help determine what is really going on?
- Are you overreacting to your parent's behavior? If so, are you willing to respond with less intensity?

———— COMING OF AGE PASSAGE ————
Shifting perspective from black and white to gray

Sending in Substitutes

Hiring temporary caregivers when you're overwhelmed does not always work to your advantage.

Ensnared by promises to keep our parents in their homes until the end, we found the search for reliable caregivers to be one of our greatest challenges, especially with regard to Impie. That quest began after a year of running back and forth between our house and hers, hoping to provide her with the security of family and preserve her savings. Feeling increasingly defeated in his efforts, John proceeded to hire and oversee a multitude of caregivers, many of whom he'd secured through networking with friends and professionals. Over the next seven years, he oriented them, mopped up after them, and washed their dishes between shifts, all the while performing general home-maintenance tasks.

The parade of hired attendants specialized in diversity. It began with Adele, who worked out well for the first two weeks until Impie became extremely agitated. In her words, she had been taken to a meeting at which she did not belong and never wanted "that woman who comes into my house" to ever frequent the premises again. Following up, John learned that Adele had been battling a drinking problem for several years, finally winning the struggle, but to maintain her sobriety she needed to attend daily AA meetings, many of which took place during the hours she supervised Impie. *Strike one.*

Next came Patsy. A registered nurse, Patsy appeared to be the answer to our prayers. She needed housing for herself and her pre-school granddaughter, a request to which John agreed, renovating a second-floor bedroom for the two of them. Patsy's compassion toward his mother had us feeling secure—until the child began tormenting Impie, kicking her under the dinner table and teasing her. Patsy was forced to choose between defending her progeny or her charge, who had taken up defense measures of her own, liberally lashing out with her cane, fingernails, or Finnish obscenities. We had to conclude that a four year old was no match for an eighty-five year old with Alzheimer's. *Strike two.*

For the next batter we went to an agency, which furnished us with a list of prescreened caregivers. After several interviews, we hired a woman who needed transportation but had solid experience. Soon she began calling in sick or just not showing up. *Foul!*

Then came a woman with body piercings who secreted things of little value from Impie's drawers. Out she went. *Ball one.*

Enter a young man, a masseuse by trade who seemed high on pot each time he visited. *Ball two.*

Next was a single mom with an infant. Impie loved holding the baby and playing with him, but unfortunately the young mother accepted a position offering more pay. *Ball three.*

Then came one of the agency's finest—Marcia, who originally wanted only daytime work but later asked to move in as she grew to love Impie and wished to increase her own income. Things went smoothly for over a year, every day of which we blessed Saint Marcia. She kept Impie uplifted and smelling fresh, and the house neat as a pin. However, Marcia started dating then wanted to move back into her own home and have more time off.

We resumed our search and, since Impie was running out of money, hoped to find someone willing to accept a reduced salary in exchange for room and board. Subsequently, a minister acquaintance recommended a homeless couple who were active in his church. Our agency, after checking for criminal backgrounds, suggested we employ them, but four months after hiring them we learned they were ex-cons. Although they were obviously committed to turning their lives around, we decided not to jeopardize Impie's state aid. *Strike three—we were out.*

Fearing that John's health might be compromised yet again, I begged him to let a geriatric care management company take over the hiring and supervision of caregivers for his mother. He agreed, still committed to keeping Impie at home, and was delighted when they engaged the services of a seasoned, middle-aged woman eager to trade part of her services for room and board. It was the depth of her caring and wisdom that helped John turn over his supervisory powers.

In the weeks following, I witnessed my husband recline into his overstuffed armchair like a triathlon victor. We were able to laugh about our hunt-and-peck campaign for assistance, in part because no one suffered significant harm and also because, reluctant to wallow in shame over poor judgment, we had managed always to salvage perspective.

Later, we learned that caregiver burnout is extremely high, especially among people who attempt day and night duty with hardly any days off. The agency with which we were working informed us that few lasted more than a year at the same job.

Had we known of this potential in advance, we would have hired a geriatric care manager much earlier, even if it necessitated rallying the family to help subsidize Impie's care. Still, we prided ourselves on following both reason and instinct rather than plowing relentlessly through this phase of caregiving.

If you need to hire in-home help . . .

If you live in an urban setting, you may have no difficulty locating quality care through a newspaper ad or an agency or private provider resource. While interviewing candidates, remember that whereas many caregivers are superb at tending to others they sometimes neglect themselves—a distinct liability since it contributes to burnout. Paying attention to potential drawbacks as well as capabilities will help you project possible scenarios.

To plan ahead for the need to hire in-home help, consider the following questions:

- Have you anticipated the kind of support your parent might require and how it will be funded?
- Have you familiarized yourself with community resources?
- What kind of network will be advising you and helping with referrals?
- Would you think about joining a support group as a first step in asking for help?
- If you are hiring in-home help yourself rather than through an agency, will you determine in advance the type of care and duties needed, design a phone interview to use for screening purposes, interview your favorite candidates in person, and scrupulously check their references?

——— COMING OF AGE PASSAGE ———
Melding logic and intuition

Twin Infernos

Occasionally going over the edge with your parent is part of
your job description as caregiver, even under the best
circumstances.

One bitter cold day when winter had lingered too long, I promised
to take my father to an adult league hockey game in which one of
his newer friends, Stan, was playing. When I picked Dad up, he
asked if he could "impose" on me to do a short grocery stop on our
way to the ice pavilion. I winced, knowing our vastly different definitions for "short," but imagined that however long this one was it
would decrease the time I would have to spend at a spectator sport
I'd never enjoyed. I also felt sure that John, although planning to
meet us at the game, would get seated and not mind the wait.

Once inside the store, Dad advised me he was fine on his own,
so I went off in search of a few items myself. Several minutes later
I noticed Dad studying a pyramid of chili con carne tins, his eyes
widening. "Finding a good deal?" I asked.

"Wow," he replied. "Thirty-nine cents a can. Think I'll get a
dozen."

Scrutinizing the label, I told him, "Dad, this chili is a dollar
thirty-nine a can."

"No it's not, Miss Know-It-All," he shot back.

Shrugging, I moved on.

Twenty minutes later, having unloaded my groceries in the car,
I returned to find him in the frozen dessert section pulling out a
half gallon of chocolate-chip mint ice cream priced at nearly six
dollars.

"Dad," I ventured, "it's probably not cold enough in the car for
ice cream to last through the game."

"Heck it isn't. The thermometer on my deck read twenty-eight
degrees this morning," he stormed.

Warning lights flashed in my mind. *It'd be easier to clean the trunk of the car than go to the mat with him. Besides, he's apt to fly into cardiac arrest when this tab gets rung up.* Biting my tongue, I urged, simply, "Better be going so we're sure to catch the second half of the game."

He agreed and ambled to the checkout counter, frozen chocolate and mint incarcerated under his arm, and I headed back to the parking lot. Through the store window, I saw him rifling through his wallet and finally handing the cashier a wad of bills. When she gave him his change, he shoved it into his pocket and exited. But once outside, he scowled then tramped back to the checkout counter and demanded a refund for the entire purchase. Empty-handed, he returned to the car cursing, "False advertising. I'll never shop there again, the crooks."

Unable to sympathize, I put on my best blank face and off we drove. As we approached a stoplight, he hollered, "J— C—, when will you learn to drive? It makes me crazy that you just roar up to a light and slam on the brakes. Get back to driver's ed, fer gawd's sake!"

Ignoring his incriminations, I waited for the green light then proceeded, reminding myself it would take only five more minutes to get to the pavilion. But Dad persisted. "I think I'll use that old bike in the garage to get around on from now on," he taunted. "I'll feel safer."

Something snapped inside me, and I jammed the brakes so hard his head nearly hit the windshield. The anger with which he consistently masked his grief had ripped fully through the matrix of my understanding. Pulling to the shoulder of the road, I shouted, "You old coot. How dare you talk to me this way!"

As we sat breathing like twin infernos, Dad asked, "Well, where'd you learn to be so angry?"

"Where do you think I learned it, Dad?" I fired back. "It wasn't from Mom!"

We drove on in silence. Not a sound was uttered until I had parked the car in the pavilion lot, trudged in the door alongside

Dad, and hunkered down in the bleachers next to John. I broke the chill with a staccato whisper: "I need to get out of here, John."

"So I noticed," he said. "Go ahead. I'll get him home after the game, honey."

Driving back, I knew I could not have contained myself during another interchange with my father since it had long before surpassed the point of no return. As the power surge raged within me, I felt a combination of shame, self-righteousness, and sadness. Still, I realized I had arrived at a crossroads, where I would no longer let him abuse me.

That night I prayed Dad would not be snatched away before we mended our altercation and that in restoring my relationship with him I could also heal myself. I fell asleep thinking about Dad's anger-coated despair and congratulating myself for refusing to relinquish essential boundaries.

If your aging parent verbally attacks you . . .

The politically correct response to a parental attack is to rise above it, but at times such action may not be possible. When instead you lose control, remember that heated situations are only a small part of your relationship with your parent and unjustified anger is probably due to frustrations originating long ago.

Repeated verbal attacks are likely to push even a saint over the edge. For support, talk to other caregivers near burnout or a trusted friend. Ideally, you can learn from your unleashed anger and then forgive yourself, knowing you have gained insight into your limitations and your parent's. To prepare for intense confrontations, consider the following questions:

- Can you admit to being angry? What might it take to acknowledge your anger?

- Are you reaching your eldercare limits or responding with unhealthy relational patterns from your childhood?

- Do you feel you have the right to protect yourself from

your parent? Do you know the difference between selfishness and self-care?

- If you are burned out as a caregiver, would you avoid potentially inflammatory conversations by seeking help or canceling or postponing activities?

- If you feel anger as a caregiver, would you join a support group, or seek assistance through counseling?

- If you lose control, can you forgive yourself, assess any damage to your relationship with your parent, and decide on preventive strategies for the future?

——— COMING OF AGE PASSAGE ———
Forgiving your negative reactions

"He Gave Her Mom's Pearl Pendant?"

Your widowed parent's romantic attachments can stir up either genuine concern within you or an urge for unbridled control.

I raised my eyebrows when, seven years after my mother's death, Dad started wearing Bay Rum aftershave. One day he muttered, "If I were half my age, I'd marry that woman. Told her so, too." The woman in question turned out to be his twenty-eight-year-old housekeeper and caregiver who cooked his breakfast and patiently followed him up and down grocery store aisles, who reminded me to refill his prescriptions, and who generally boosted my sanity when I had reached my limit with caregiving.

While a part of me was apprehensive, another part revolted, thinking, *But Dad is in his nineties. How can he possibly consider a nuptial, especially with a woman one-third his age? He's still so in love with my mother he would never replace her with someone new, and if he tries to, his ancient heart will give out before he ever makes it to the altar.*

A month later, the caregiver called to say Dad had given her Mom's pearl pendant–the brooch he had presented to Mom as a pre-engagement gift. The caregiver assured me she would return it since that was the only right thing to do but pleaded with me not to mention a word to Dad so his feelings would not be hurt. I agreed, relieved to avoid another daughter-father confrontation and grateful to be informed of the transaction.

Even so, protectiveness and fear danced in the shadows of my mind, where my father belonged with my mother and no one else. My head filled with judgments about elderly men marrying young women, and I tried to imagine Dad being one of those trophy-bride guys. Then I flashed on the caregiver's motive, wondering if she was a gold digger. Surely she couldn't have affection for Dad, who had dentures, could scarcely see, wore the same musty clothes day after day, refusing to throw out old worn shirts, and told the same stories repeatedly. No way, I thought–but worry lingered.

Appealing to my brothers, I was surprised to find them not at all alarmed at the news, and in fact somewhat amused by it. One commented, "Well, maybe the old boy still has it," while the other said, "You know, he's probably having fun with this." Though they expressed apprehension about his rationale, neither offered to don military fatigues and stave off what I saw as an impending disaster. Even John flashed a smile.

As weeks passed, I saw that behind my protectiveness and fear, nostalgia had set up camp in my head. And there it remained until I was willing to let tears flow, releasing my picture-perfect images of Mom and Dad. In the space they had occupied, I began to understand my father's loneliness and yearning. I recalled how he had relished the touch of a masseuse a few months after Mom's death and how I'd once caught him dancing to Dixieland jazz with an old mannequin Mom had used for her sewing projects. *No matter how old one gets*, I concluded, *the need for sensuality and intimacy lives on.*

Consequently, I relinquished the task of compiling an Owner's Operating Manual for those I loved most and instead began responding to situations as openheartedly as possible. This meant letting go of my need to control outcomes and trusting that people I cherished would be guided by their own intelligence as well as a gentle spirit.

Soon after, Dad was in midsentence describing his relationship with his caregiver when suddenly his mind and body gave out. Perhaps he had merely wanted to have a place of pleasure to go in his mind, or maybe he really loved this woman and looked forward to combining care and affection under the same roof. The one thing I knew for sure was that the joy he derived from his relationship helped stand him in good stead as he prepared his exit.

If your parent has a prospective mate . . .

When an aging widowed parent begins courting, dangerous flames may not engulf you, but you can still smell the smoke. The more perilous blazes generally erupt earlier in life, posing the prospect of stepfamily living or a mate you disapprove of; your parent's religious conversion, abandoned friendships, or uncomfortable financial arrangements; or your parent's decreased availability. Now, facing your parent's late-life romance, a part of you might instead feel ensnared in childhood and threatened by insecurity.

For a more realistic perception of the situation, seek advice from other family members and friends. Also try empathizing with your parent's need for companionship. To better prepare for the likelihood that your aging parent will kindle a new love, consider the following questions:

• Does your parent tend to make wise decisions? Would professional help be advisable?

• Are you willing to acknowledge your inner responses to your parent's courtship activities, let go of what was, and make peace with new developments?

• Can you shift your perspective enough to stop micro-managing your parent's life and begin supporting their ultimate happiness?

• If your parent becomes romantically involved with a care-giver, might you react negatively? How will you know if the negativity is your problem or if it's no longer appropriate for the individual to be serving in a professional capacity? Who should make this decision?

———— COMING OF AGE PASSAGE ————
Staring down emotional reactions

English as a Second Language

The language of professionals can spin anyone into a web of confusion.

In the beginning, we surmised it was only our parents who needed a glossary while interfacing with medical and legal experts. We caught ourselves snickering when my dad said, "Yep, my lawyer explained one of those 'doable powers' where they give the attorney the right to make all your decisions for you. I don't want one of those; I'm sure as heck not going to deal with someone who is only interested in getting my money. And I'm not going to pay for an 'advance directory' that might not get here till after I die."

But as we increased our involvement in parental caregiving, it became apparent that we were just as stymied by the terminology of professionals. Whenever we forgot to request that unfamiliar terms be translated into plain English, the notes we took either drove us to the dictionary or kept us from finding solutions to problems. Though familiar with the concepts of "durable power of attorney" and "advance directive," we were left in the dust by "palliative care" and "intestacy," the convoluted vernacular used to describe the easing of symptoms and not having a valid will. We exchanged puzzled glances when a doctor asked if Impie was being "hydrated," only to discover his inquiry had nothing to do with hooking her up to a hose but rather with giving her fluids. And we were relieved to discover "ADLs" was not a disease but instead the acronym for "activities of daily living"—one of the assessments used to measure a senior's need for support.

Interpreting the risks for treatments or procedures about which doctors are legally bound to inform patients was equally confounding and sometimes frightening, such as when a physician said, "One of the extremely low risks of this procedure is that we could accidentally hit an artery and cause internal bleeding." Other times it was disconcerting when physicians overly minimized potential consequences. For example, as Dad faced a prostate biopsy and possible surgery, a doctor warned him he might experience a little discomfort. Hearing this, John told me, "A little discomfort, my eye! When they go through the urethra, it will hurt like hell. My buddy Rudy's biopsy hurt so much he was sure his genitalia would soon drop off."

Linguistic confusion taunted us while researching the housing industry, as well. Retirement communities, for example, were licensed as boarding homes in some instances and Continuing Care Retirement Communities (CCRCs) in others, implying the additional provisions of assisted living and skilled nursing services; at times, a retirement facility was instead termed a "senior apartment." As for the difference between a skilled nursing facility (SNF) and a nursing home, we learned the former often affords more technical medical equipment or specialty services.

If you or your parent is struggling with terminology associated with services for elders . . .

For a quick tutorial in terminology, see Eldercare Glossary, pages 253–259. To turn a common stumbling block into a stepping stone, learn to differentiate Medicare (federal health insurance covering certain services for people over age sixty-five who qualify for Social Security) from Medicaid (state medical assistance for those qualified because of financial need). Read the fine print for each of these programs since the benefits and requirements can change from year to year; literature is available through your local Area Agency on Aging and other community senior service providers. To postpone dependence on state help, you may want to purchase supplemental insurance, often referred to as Medigap insurance. See the Partnership for Clear Health Communication, sponsored by the American Medical Association and American Public Health Administration, for more tips on narrowing the doctor-patient communication gap.

In addition to these resources, you can enhance your ability to deal with services for elders by considering the following questions:

- Are you diligently seeking clarification of terms and services you do not understand?
- Have you asked your parent about accompanying them to appointments if they are experiencing confusion or fear, and also to complex diagnostic procedures or treatment?
- Are you familiar with social service agencies and support groups in your community that can help you elucidate the language and ideology of eldercare?

——— COMING OF AGE PASSAGE ———

Acknowledging there are no simple solutions

"If You Think It's Not Safe for Me to Drive, Just Tell Me!"

You may be amazed at the power struggles and deceit propelled by the threatened loss of driving privileges.

My father's diagnosis of glaucoma substantiated my concern about his deteriorating ability to drive. Since he did not volunteer to quit and his eye doctor had never advised him to, I knew I'd need to take a firm stand. Uncomfortable with confrontations, I procrastinated until waking up from a third nightmare about a tragedy caused by Dad's driving. I asked him, "Dad, if at some point it seems unwise for you to continue driving, what would you like me to do?" He replied in a sincere tone, "If you think it's not safe for me to drive, just tell me!"

So I told him. He went ballistic, pulling out an entire arsenal of intimidation tactics. I backpedaled to three years of age, becoming so flustered I wondered if I'd be able to drive home from the doctor's office. When we were both battle-fatigued, Dad agreed not to drive anymore.

A week later, I found his refrigerator filled with fresh food. I countered by disabling his car. Furious, he called in the mobile repair service and hit the road again.

Days later, my friend Margaret reported she had seen his white Hyundai straddling two lanes on the main drag in town. "It was awful!" she moaned. "He had a huge parade of honking cars behind him." Confronting Dad, I threatened to take the car away; he retaliated with, "I'll take you to court."

When the temperature cooled, I demanded he stop driving. He told me he had lost the keys, so it wouldn't be an issue anymore. But less than three days later I noticed a streak of gray paint on his car and cornered him. Not only did he deny having driven, he swore he had no clue how the stripe had gotten there.

I suggested he enroll in a school for older drivers; he refused. So I tracked down the keys and sequestered the car, parking it in front of our house. It was a chilly seven months before the thaw set in.

If you have concerns about your parent's driving ability . . .

Few subjects are as charged as determining whether or not a parent needs to hang up the car keys. While some elders are unsafe on the road, others are skilled drivers with health complications that require them to surrender their driving privileges. Ideally, they will make this decision on their own. If they don't, their adult children may feel called upon to build a case against them, appeal to medical professionals, or insist on turning decisions over to the state's licensing department. Even then, it is a parent's right to risk driving provided that they are mentally competent.

If your parent is having trouble with vision–especially depth perception–is grappling with memory loss or impaired reactions, or is using mind-altering pharmaceuticals or misusing alcohol, and your family decides to conduct an intervention, plan carefully. Since your parent may potentially harm themselves or others, timing is paramount. Speak honestly, relay concern without judgment, and show how the cessation of driving will decrease your parent's stress levels and increase their safety.

Even so, your parent may not be easily persuaded. Before taking action, ask yourself the following questions:

- Is there a strong basis for concern about your parent's safety while driving, and do others share your perception?

- Given what you understand about your parent's personality, what is your most effective intervention strategy and source of support? Are you prepared for consequences that could undermine your relationship with your parent?

- Are there viable alternatives to terminating your parent's mobility, such as requiring the use of assistive devices or establishing agreed upon limits on driving activity? If your parent stops driving, have you arranged for their future transportation needs?

- Are you aware of your state's license renewal guidelines for the elderly?

———— COMING OF AGE PASSAGE ————
Putting your parent-child relationship at risk

PART 3 ———
Letting Go

As your experience with eldercare continues, you may find that unable to outdistance the demons of change, you can only be saved by letting go—but of what? Jobs? (Maybe.) Marriage? (Not necessarily.) Money? (Perhaps.) Sanity? (Yes, but only temporarily.) Identity? (Sure, but that will change anyway.)

Worn down by grief, you may no longer be able to avoid the "little deaths" suffered on the way to losing a parent. Perhaps you will also begin looking a bit scruffy, discovering a sock from the dryer stuck in your shirt while conducting a workshop, for example, or forgetting to zipper up or tweeze or floss. Moreover, your usually sharp mind may jump a synapse, your body may stumble, your spirit dip.

To cope, some individuals weep openly, while others jog or journal. Now and then it helps to rage—beating rubber gloves against the kitchen counter or pounding a mattress—rather than turning pent-up anger against yourself or loved ones. In response, the Pied Piper of childhood may sigh, suggesting it is time to wake up as an adult "in the mourning."

The consummate try-harder couple, John and I tenaciously entertained images of our intact parents, enhancing our denial of their eventual demise. We read up on nutrition and exercise, barraging our parents with information we hoped would help them remain the people we had always known. But they had other ideas, like eating handfuls of Hershey Kisses at a sitting or playing Russian roulette with their finances. Only when we saw the impossibility of willing a change in our parents' behavior could the dialogue begin. Then, with newfound humility and increased respect, we recognized that how they looked, ate, acted, and lived their lives were really their decisions, as long as they were competent to make them. At that point, we were finally able to admit our parents were fading and would some day leave us behind.

In eldercare, letting go occurs only when you are too pooped to hang on any longer, when your creativity is tapped and your mind unable to conjure up yet another "more viable" approach. It is possible to become quite adept at letting go provided that, in the interest of healing, there is one thing you retain: a sense of humor that allows for sacrilege.

"Transfer the Money!"

If your parent holds financial affairs close to the chest, it's never too early to start asking questions.

A few months after our marriage in 1964, we received a call at our Seattle apartment from John's mother Impie, in Spokane, saying, "I don't want to alarm you, but the doctors have found cancer in Dad's stomach and he needs immediate surgery." Though Ray had been plagued by illness for years, we were stunned by the C word. As it turned out, he survived the procedure but remained in ill health. Dependent and unable to work, he stayed as upbeat as possible by reading extensively and watching television.

Within five years of this crisis, we moved back to our hometown of Spokane, in part to be nearby while Ray's health was failing. Years later John, the only sibling in town, tried to discuss end-of-life planning with him, emphasizing that if Ray became an invalid or passed away, John would be responsible for Impie's well-being. Ray replied that everything was taken care of and returned to the Lawrence Welk show he had been watching.

Remembering his dad had recently fantasized about buying a Mercedes-Benz and driving to Sedona, Arizona, for the winter, John pursued the discussion from a new angle. "Dad, thus far we've been able to activate state and federal support for you and Mom because you qualify as a couple," he said. "But for a single person, the funding requirements change radically. I wouldn't have a clue about how to proceed because I don't know where you stand financially. If you have stocks or bonds stashed away, they could be added to your checking account so the money can go toward Mom's care. But if you're thinking of traveling south for the cold season, it seems you'd first have to unearth a little nest egg you've got hidden away. Is this something you want to tell me about?"

"Nope," Ray retorted, closing this avenue of communication.

A few months later, Ray was carried by ambulance attendants to the ER with John by his side. Ray suddenly rose and, waving a forefinger above his head, implored, "Transfer the money!" No sooner did John ask, "What money?" than Ray drifted into oblivion, remaining comatose for six days then dying.

Afterward, John and his brothers turned their father's house upside down in search of the money, but to no avail. Only coincidentally did they find a financial adviser's rumpled business card in a billfold that had been stashed in a bag for Goodwill and, after calling, recover $20,000 that had been in a money market account—an amount that nearly subsidized Impie's expenses over several years until she died. Many months later, while turning the mattress in preparation for Aunt Lyna's stay in Ray's former bedroom, John discovered his father's financial records in the bedsprings.

If you are not fully cognizant of your parent's financial situation . . .

Though money is often considered a private matter, one of the most stressful issues in caregiving is not knowing your parent's financial situation and thus being unable to plan for various care contingencies. The best way to address this problem is through communicating with your parents about their finances. Such exchanges are often perceived as risky because adult children see their parents' financial affairs as off-limits, wish to avoid thinking about a parent's illness or death, and quake at the thought of appearing interested in inheritance.

But don't let any of these misgivings thwart the critical conversations you have as a family. With Ray, we waited so long we learned nothing about his investments and insurance coverage. Had we familiarized ourselves with his financial assets before his health started to deteriorate, we could have spared ourselves much anguish, as well as the money we contributed to Impie's expenses prior to discovering Ray's funds.

To start gathering financial information in preparation for the illness or death of a parent, consult Appendix A, "Financial and Legal Matters," pages 214–215, and consider the following questions:

- Do you know where your parent's financial documents are stored or the identity of their financial advisers?
- Are you aware of any concerns your parent may have about their financial future or of their plans to cover expenses as they age?
- If your parent refuses to discuss finances with you, are they willing to share the names of financial or legal advisers with whom they've worked, or describe assets including the value of possessions or property?
- Have you asked your parent if in the future they might be financially dependent on you or other members of the family, so you can plan ahead?
- Do you have a durable power of attorney that addresses the finances that are in place for your parent?

——— COMING OF AGE PASSAGE ———

Replacing erroneous beliefs with new information

Packing for the Final Journey

Understanding that your parent will never be the same as before takes perspective and special skills.

John was hell-bent on making his mother Impie understand the illogic of her emergent behaviors. Attached like Velcro to the medical concept that a diagnosis of Alzheimer's can be substantiated only by a brain biopsy after death, he was sure she remained the mentally sound mother he had always known. So when he stopped by Impie's place one day to find her hammering exposed nail heads on her hardwood floors he was speechless. Having maneuvered a massive rolltop desk nearly thirty-feet from its original position, she was revved up and reeking of body odor. John blinked in disbelief, sat beside her on the floor, and said, "Mom, we can hire someone to do this. Or I can work on it next weekend. Why don't you slow down and jump in the tub."

"Leave me alone!" she shouted.

A few weeks later, he noticed Impie's clothes were beginning to hang on her. *Good, she could stand to lose about fifty pounds,* he mused. But soon after, he learned she was losing weight because her hardwiring for cooking had become defective and she was forgetting about meals.

Then, hearing from his brothers that she had accused him of stealing money, John confronted Impie, who denied the charges. Worried she would lose or hide a large amount of cash, he provided her weekly with a twenty-dollar bill in lieu of the eighty-dollar monthly installments to which she was accustomed. "This isn't enough, and it's my money," she would challenge. John found that when he ignored her pleas the storm would eventually pass.

Soon he felt as if his life was punctuated with drive-by shootings. Impie started begging to go "home," though John assured her she was already there. When an African-American woman came to care for her, Impie showered her with a litany of racial slurs, causing the aide to resign.

Impie also adopted a packing fetish, hauling suitcases from the attic to her bedroom and stuffing them with clothes. When John came across the luggage, he tried suppressing his anger, saying, "Mom, you're not going anywhere. Please stop this ridiculous packing." But the incessant packing continued, whereupon John hid the luggage in the garage, prompting Impie to use plastic grocery bags instead. John was about to give up when another aide suggested taking most of his mother's clothes to the basement, leaving just a few items for her to pack.

Next, Impie stated she was no longer going to attend classes at Day Health, where she had been enrolled for recreational and therapeutic purposes. Aware of her fear of confrontation, John announced, "Well, you'll have to tell the bus driver you're not going today." Rather than face the discomfort, she agreed to get on the van.

Another incident occurred when, while phoning Impie from a conference, John heard her sob, "I have lost my husband, and I am all alone." John immediately left the seminar to be with her, but this time, instead of trying to modify her reality he allowed her to grieve. After crying, she whispered, "I know this will sound really strange, but I believe your dad visited me earlier and was sitting with me in the kitchen." Less skeptical than usual, John thought, *Maybe this really did happen . . . what do I know anyway?* One thing he did know, at long last, was that Alzheimer's had taken over and there was no stopping it.

He began to accept the idea that the mother he had known would never come back. To fight the sadness welling within him, he spent hours a day watching television; gradually he began sitting quietly in his favorite chair, crying. Seeing that his mother's disease was not within his jurisdiction, John ultimately let go of his urge to maintain the status quo.

If logic isn't working with your aging parent . . .

It can be difficult to accept that a parent is dying while still living, that though the physical body remains, mentally, emotionally, and spiritually the person has changed beyond recognition. You may be tempted to let your parent's relatively unimpaired physical appearance distract you from their diminishing mental capacity. Or you may simply pretend things are not as bad as they seem. In either instance, with repeated interactions you can gradually come to understand that your parent may never behave as in the past.

After surrendering to the inevitable, it is possible to learn better ways of communicating with an aging parent. To discover your parent's needs, for example, you could mirror their words and behavior back to them, joining in their delusion rather than attempting to convince them their facts are incorrect. If your parent is worried, you could console them or address their real fears, dealing with your own emotions later. Every connection you make with your parent's reality can reduce anxiety levels for both of you.

To help prepare for the difficulties encountered when a parent loses the capacity to be logical and responsible for their behavior, consider the following questions:

- Are you are in denial about your parent's condition? If so, what behavior supports the possibility of an altered reality? How can you learn to accept this reality?

- Do you need help expressing grief? Where can you get such help?

- Can you to surrender to the will of whatever you believe controls the fate of the dying, whether it is God, a higher power, or nature? How might you develop the perspective necessary for surrender—through journaling, reading an inspirational book, or creating a ritual?

—— COMING OF AGE PASSAGE ——
Surrendering to little deaths

"We'll Put It in Nice, Fat Curls . . ."

Moments of comic relief might appear from nowhere when you most need them.

After my mother's third week in the nursing home, her best friend pulled me aside during a visit and said, "Gail, I would like to pay for your mom to get a haircut at that little salon down the hall." I studied Mom, noticing her bangs had grown past her eyebrows and a mane was trailing down her back.

"My gosh, Lenora, you're right. I'll take care of it," I blurted out, embarrassed about the oversight. But in the background I could see Mom nodding vigorously from side to side. Approaching her bed, I asked, "Are you saying you don't want a haircut?"

Her frown reaffirmed my interpretation.

"Well, how about if I wash your hair?" Mom paused, slowly nodding permission.

I returned later with a bottle of shampoo, surrounded her with towels for drips, and got to work. She rolled her eyes as I lathered the thin scalp that cloaked the mischief of misfiring neurons and gasping vessels. All at once, she grabbed my arm and laughed, "Curls . . . *big!*"

Mom was remembering when she had been the hairdresser and I was ten years old. She had unwound rods from my hair as we held our breath to see if the permanent had taken. As always, I looked like a Curly Kate scouring pad, but this particular time it was worse, every hair resembling the letter *z*. Horrified, I reminded her how we handled train-wrecked permanents: "Mom, please tell me you'll set it in nice fat curls and it will be all right in a couple of weeks." This she did, and in two weeks my coiffeur simmered down.

Now in the nursing home, with Mom's death inching closer like floodwater, my eyes crinkled, and I quoted her: "It's okay, honey. We'll put in nice fat curls, and it will be just fine."

As she squeezed my hand, we giggled, soon crossing the threshold between laughter and tears. Wiping our eyes, we heard chuckles from both sides of the hallway. One chorus came from the room of a ninety-three-year-old resident who spent four hours each day hollering, "You've got to help me!" Snickers also came from a woman who during the same four hours bellowed back, "Shut up! You're driving me crazy."

When I saw Mom the next day, her eyes enveloped me with warmth instead of the usual depression. And though she sometimes seemed discouraged, there remained a palpable bond between us that lasted for the rest of her short life.

If you're worried about being disrespectful by using humor . . .

Chances are your sense of humor will evolve dramatically as your caregiving role becomes more demanding. John and I would never have survived our stint as caregivers without cultivating opportunities to laugh, all the while acknowledging the seriousness of our families' circumstances and respecting our parents' ordeals. We came to believe that a component of faith is chuckling at yourself and trusting all will be well.

Instead of feeling guilty about seeing humor in serious situations, realize that laughter can boost your mental health and thus promote better caregiving. When caregivers become immobilized by grief and depression, the people they care for also are negatively affected. To evaluate how humor affects caregiving, consider the following questions:

- Looking back over your eldercare experience, do you see situations that did not seem funny at the time but do now?

- Do you understand the concept of laughing *with* rather than *at?*

- If you feel you have misjudged the appropriateness of humor while caregiving, can you forgive yourself and make amends to your parent?

——— COMING OF AGE PASSAGE ———
Welcoming the bonds of humor

"Oh My God, I've Killed My Mom!"

Making an end-of-life decision may seem like you are killing a parent.

When time passed and my mother showed no improvement after her second stroke, we all agreed it was time to let her go, a decision that meant giving her comfort but no nourishment, hydration, or oxygen. Ironically, the next day Mom's eyes sparkled and she was able to sit up in bed. Panicking, I began to sob and thought, *Oh my God, I've killed my mom!* Then fearing I would upset her more by failing to regain my composure, I drew a chair to her bed, held her hand, and whispered, "It's okay, Mom."

Coincidentally, I heard an overhead page for Dr. Jim Shaw, a friend of the family. Right away I called the hospital operator, asking if Dr. Shaw could come to Mom's room. When he arrived, he pieced together the situation and explained, "Your daughter is concerned about the decision the family has made on your behalf, Jeanne. These days we're learning a lot more about dying, and it seems that when someone is getting ready to die they often appear to be getting better. This has been a very difficult decision for your family, even though they know it's what you would want. Can you squeeze my hand if you want to be allowed to die?" Mom clenched Jim's hand.

He continued, "Because you seem so animated, they fear you are trying to hang on to life, and they have cut off some medical support that might facilitate recovery. Do you understand?" Mom squeezed his hand again.

Then Jim turned to me and said, "Gail, you know in your heart you've done the right thing. Now she's in God's hands—and so are you. Can you let your mother go?"

"Yes," I cried, nuzzling my cheek against hers. Two days later, Mom died quietly—a delicate vapor slipping away.

With Mom, the decision for "no heroic measures" was especially difficult because her second stroke had come on unexpectedly and when she was still so young. At that point, John and I, acquiescing to my parents' need to dodge reality, had not yet engaged them in tough talks about the inevitable. Emboldened by this experience, however, we were better prepared for the next death of a parent in our family.

If you fear making a decision to let your parent go . . .

Participation in the dying of a loved one can be a privilege for all involved since it is one of life's most intense and profound experiences. To reduce the likelihood of fear, reflect ahead of time on potential end-of-life decisions that might have to be made in various circumstances and explore their emotional impact. In addition, attempt to understand the technicalities of life-support systems. It is also possible to draw courage from the experiences of others, by joining a support group or reading biographies of people who have had to face difficult end-of-life decisions.

The desire to support your parent's end-of-life wishes can be best fulfilled if you are fully cognizant of their preferred death experience. To better prepare for this circumstance before a crisis arises, consider the following questions:

- Have you discussed your parent's end-of-life wishes with them?

- Do you accept you can never be 100 percent sure about the "rightness" of decisions you make concerning your parent's death experience?

- Do you feel comfortable alleviating fears through prayer and meditation? Are you aware of supportive resources available through other spiritual practices, friends, relatives, religious institutions, or community agencies and organizations?

- Are you willing to do all you can to ensure the integrity of your parent's death and then let go?

"What Isn't Clear about 'No CPR'?"

Even with power of attorney or guardianship, denying end-of-life support for your parent is a monumental decision.

On an Alzheimer's sojourn of no return, John's mother Impie had mentally emigrated to another place and time. She avoided conversation, and we gauged her feelings by watching her pack and unpack her suitcases.

Seeing her caught in the web of this progressive and fatal disease, John attained guardianship of her, including obtaining a No CPR (no cardiovascular or pulmonary resuscitation) order from Impie's physician, who had diagnosed her as terminally ill. This directive, commonly referred to as a Do Not Resuscitate (DNR) instruction or a No Code request, reflected wishes she had expressed prior to her spiraling into Alzheimer's. As advised, John posted the form on the refrigerator door for the benefit of caregivers or anyone else involved in a decision to let her die.

One Friday evening weeks later, we slipped out of the caregiving loop for dinner, a movie, and oblivion sans cell phone.

Arriving home about 9:00 p.m., we found a phone message from Impie's caregiver reporting that Impie had been suddenly unresponsive, and unable to reach us, the attendant had dialed 911. However, when the paramedics arrived she had failed to call their attention to the directive on the refrigerator. As a result, Impie had been delivered to the intensive care unit at a downtown hospital and immediately connected to an IV.

We raced to the ICU, where the physician on duty told us, "We don't think she'll make it through the evening. I suggest you contact family members."

"Why is she hooked up to tubes?" John asked.

"We are hydrating her for comfort," said the physician.

"We have a No CPR order in place," John explained.

"Then why did you send her to the hospital?" asked the physician.

Because we assumed Impie would be gone before the night was over, the fact that the directive had not been followed hardly mattered. But three days later Impie was discharged from the hospital, after which she proceeded to live two more years in the increasingly impenetrable fog of her disease.

The experience showed us how little we knew about interfacing with the medical system. Though we recognized that legal documents like an advance directive, durable power of attorney, and No CPR instruction were cornerstones of final planning activities, we had no idea that a document substantiating a parent's wish to avoid heroic measures could have limitations. When we interviewed the caregiver about why she didn't show this form to the paramedics, she said she hadn't been able to find it. Later, we learned that even if she had, there was no guarantee it would be honored in the event that doubts lurked in the minds of the paramedics. In addition, we naively assumed that if someone on the verge of death was taken to the ER, professional staff would determine whether death was imminent, and if it was, the patient would be transferred immediately to a hospital room.

Nor were we aware of the legal intricacies of entering a hospital. Although Impie had been serviced by hospice and returned home under its wing, we did not know that her hospice contact person should have been called at the outset—a move that could have prevented her trip to the hospital. Someone not in the care of hospice who arrives at a hospital in need of pain management, on the other hand, might be referred to hospice. If the family declines to follow through, the hospital staff may either treat the patient or arrange for nursing-home care. In the interim, if certain criteria are unmet the patient can be decertified by Medicare or disqualified from insurance coverage, making it necessary for them to pay privately for the hospital expenses incurred.

Similarly, ethical considerations were beyond the scope of our understanding. We have since spoken with oncologists who counsel patients' families to consider the many possible outcomes of hospitalization, inferring that a kind of domino effect could propel a patient toward an unwanted fate, as in the adage "The cure is sometimes worse than the disease." For someone whose quality of life is already extremely impaired, treatment in the hospital can be far less tolerable than pain management at home.

If your parent's nonheroic end-of-life planning might go awry . . .

If you are grappling with the possibility of denying end-of-life support for your parent, be aware that many adult children who are clear about intent become confused by emotion as a parent approaches death. Consequently, it is important to understand beforehand the various implications likely to be introduced by the medical system.

In particular, be mindful that the protocol for handling a No CPR instruction can vary substantially from one community to another in terms of housing arrangement, emergency system, and coroner responses. For instance, boarding homes in the state of Washington are mandated to call 911 if a resident is in crisis, regardless of preferences stated by the resident or family member. Further, physicians on staff at some skilled nursing facilities routinely override No CPR and No Code requests. To understand the norms in your area, contact your parent's physician or the local medical examiner's or coroner's office.

Additionally, it is wise to select a qualified mentor who can counsel you through the steps involved in dealing with the death of a loved one. Preferably, choose someone capable of assisting with the many details that, if overlooked, can needlessly complicate your experience. If your parent qualifies for aid through hospice or another agency licensed to handle end-of-life procedures, reach out to them for support through this transition.

End-of-life planning for a parent is never actually complete until the parent has died, at which point other priorities come to the fore. To prepare for the eventual death of a parent opting for a No CPR directive, consider the following questions:

- Does your family agree with your parent's end-of-life preferences? If not, is the power of attorney amenable to honoring your parent's wishes amidst potential controversy?

- In a crisis involving your parent, if you can't be reached immediately who is your backup decision-maker?

- Are you aware of professionals who can counsel you through the affordability and logic of hospital care, as well as difficult decisions about extending life versus allowing for death?

——— COMING OF AGE PASSAGE ———
Acknowledging limitations of control

Economist in the Kitchen

When your parent takes a creative approach to cooking, frugality can outweigh nutrition and even expiration dates.

Over time, my father lost weight, resulting in dentures that no longer fit. Unwilling to purchase new ones, he transitioned to a softer diet, and though I offered to prepare his meals, he insisted on doing his own cooking. Dad's signature breakfast consisted of instant oatmeal with a splash of milk, and a glass of slightly fermented orange juice. His favorite lunch concoction was Tomato Soup for Only Pennies—made by combining a small can of tomato sauce with two tablespoons of water and a dash of Worcestershire sauce.

Sometimes Dad's evening meal boasted a hamburger patty, seasoned and seared, then folded between two slices of aging bread and garnished with a pickle. As time went on, dinner menus featured Mushroom Soup Surprise, Egg Foo Chili, and Vienna Sausage-Potato. Bypassing refrigeration, each was recycled for breakfast—laden with bacteria we prayed would not acclimate to its new host. Until then, and usually afterward as well, Dad's kitchen was strewn with wreckage from memory lapses, including scorched potholders and charred frying pans. As a result, I lived in fear that he would become a permanent patron of the ER if he didn't first burn down the house.

Delighted with his improvisations, Dad often saved a spoonful for me. But remembering his aversion to hand washing, I'd politely refuse, claiming I'd just finished a meal myself. He'd look disappointed and begin discussing the national economy, lecturing me about how little it had cost him to eat during the Great Depression and admonishing me for not clipping coupons. Despite the potential for disaster, everyone and everything survived Dad's adventures in the kitchen.

If your parent's approaches to domestic tasks seem risky . . .

As parents fight to maintain their autonomy, they sometimes take on activities for which they have little expertise, adopting attitudes of deprivation or indulgence. When the scales tip toward potential disaster, intervention becomes necessary. However, the line separating safety concerns from your parent's need for dignity can be fuzzy, causing you to vacillate between compassion and tough love. You can help avert disaster by learning basic safety precautions and discussing them with your parent. But since it is difficult to force a parent into changing their lifestyle, at some point you will have to dismiss your worries and hope for the best. For example, if you've offered to cook or to clear the roof of pine needles and encounter a stubborn refusal, give yourself credit for trying and, unless the risks are serious, pray the outcome won't be catastrophic and that you will survive your personal hell if it is.

To prepare for remaining levelheaded yet empathic with a fiercely independent parent, consider the following questions:

- Do you understand the forces that shape your parent's value system?

- If your parent is unwilling to change risky behaviors, under what circumstances would you give up? When would you take over? From whom could you get advice and support, if necessary?

- Would you be able to forgive yourself and your parent in the event of unfortunate consequences?

———— COMING OF AGE PASSAGE ————
Recognizing your way is not the only way

On Parent Patrol

You can't expect success as a food cop for your parent.

I was there when the doctor told my father, "It's critical to restrict your salt intake. Can you do that?"

Dad nodded and gave a testimonial about his good behavior: "Yep. I have really been watching it—using that salt substitute and everything."

I was there the next day, too, while Dad feasted on a Beanie-Weenie combo, saltshaker in hand. Without a trace of guilt, he invited me to join him. "Do you want to have a stroke, Dad?" I asked. "The amount of sodium in your lunch today can't help but elevate your blood pressure, aggravate your heart disease, and increase your fluid retention. And recently I've noticed you're devouring chocolate, making your ankles swell again."

When it became clear I was getting nowhere, I appealed to other family members, all of whom agreed to suggest slowing down on the salt during their weekly calls to him. As it turned out, he just went through the motions of consent when they raised the topic. Meanwhile, I envisioned planting a hidden camera on Dad's premises to provide ammunition for my next lecture and composed threats about mailing my findings to his doctor.

Several weeks later Dad's congestive heart condition worsened, and with remorse my youngest brother observed, "You know, it's impossible to convince him that his eating habits might be compromising his health. We've advised him of all the known consequences, and so has his heart specialist. Why not let him do what he wants?"

Though Dad's decision to continue ingesting salt appeared bullheaded, I had to agree the choice was his to make. His behavior may have compromised his health, but most often it seemed to enhance his quality of life because it gave him pleasure and preserved his dignity.

If your parent refuses to adhere to medical restrictions . . .

Parents of sound mind have a right to self-determination and, as such, might decide to take risks. Initially, all you can do if your parent overrides medical advice is share your feelings and concerns. If later you decide to strong-arm a situation, choose your battles carefully and realize there can be consequences for pushing. Otherwise, let go, and if you become plagued by guilt following a parental decision that has complicated your parent's illness or shortened their life, allow for grief.

To determine a strategy for coping with a parent who refuses to heed medical advice, consider the following questions:

- Can you accept that your influence over your parent is limited?

- If you can't bear watching behavior that contradicts medical advice, are you willing to learn to live with it? Or can you appeal to professionals and others for support?

- Are you prepared for criticism if you choose not to force your parent to comply with sound advice?

———— COMING OF AGE PASSAGE ————
Doing the kind thing

Psychodrama in the Backyard

Your aging parent might express themselves in ways that are perplexing—but also enlightening.

My mother was always happiest outdoors. When her grandchildren were preschoolers, she concocted a "yellow brick road" amidst the tangle of hollyhocks in her garden. Fashioned out of miniature boulders raked from beneath the dirt, the pathway engaged the children's imaginations and alerted them to treasures of the earth, as was her hope.

Dad, on the other hand, seemed more comfortable within the confines of their home—until Mom died. Then my agoraphobic father began to venture beyond the back porch, risking exposure to mosquitoes, gabby neighbors, and extremes in the weather, eventually learning to love rocks himself.

Failing to recall Mom's retrieval of the stones from beneath the soil, Dad believed them to have been divinely placed on the property and so unique that he began searching through geology books to identify them. Soon, he arranged a display of stones speckled with mica or shaped by erosion. The signage read, "Assembled by Professor C. Gladder, Archaeologist," one of many titles Dad had invented to heighten his stature while straying toward unfamiliar subject matter.

One summer afternoon while sitting together on the back porch, I detected a pile of brown lumps baking in the sun and asked, "What are those, Dad?"

Avoiding the questions in my eyes, he replied, "They're my rocks. I painted them brown. Gonna make a sculpture out of them."

Days later there appeared a unisex figurine christened "Madame Pooh" and sprouting the sawed-off arms of Mom's mannequin, spray-painted black, adorned with white evening gloves, and sporting a spigot at its waist. A cutout caricature of Teddy

Roosevelt topped the mound, while a small jug at its feet bore the painted insignia "XXX."

While visiting, the grandchildren were forgiving in their analysis, though it was difficult for them to hide their dismay. "Tell us about this, Papa," grandson Greg urged. Since the best Dad could offer was a cursory description of the details, we started feeling a little uneasy about his state of mind as reflected by this Rorschach. Despite my every attempt to mine its significance, all I could conclude was the sculpture had been his attempt at giving final expression to a time in which he had lived and the nature of his personal struggles.

Next, Dad created collages out of photographs torn from albums and pictures clipped from magazines. In one, he glued a picture of Rod Steiger next to his own photograph then framed the two together. The tie-in seemed at first to be two bald pates, but perhaps went deeper, I mused, after reading about Steiger's advocacy for the rights of the mentally ill—a category for which Dad easily qualified, along with myself and other family members battling depression.

Viewing the collages, I struggled to fathom the paradoxes they expressed. Within beauty Dad had found ugliness; within the repulsive, compassion. His statements of prejudice conveyed the love he felt for disadvantaged children; his propaganda revealed his own character defects. Finally I understood how the collision of irreconcilable opposites had helped him reach truth.

Two years after Dad's death, I am still discovering "love notes" he left each of his family members, with instructions to be opened after his death. Concealed in drawers, file cabinets, and his golf bag, they were meant to ensure that his affection and gratitude would be felt fully by each recipient.

If you are confused about your parent's attempts to communicate symbolically . . .

The contradictions and incongruities inherent in creative expression can make it difficult to understand what an aging parent might be trying to articulate. These modes of expression neverthe-less provide many opportunities for learning more about a parent's background and character. With interpretation they can, like inkblot tests, disclose hidden traits and other information valuable to an understanding of a parent before they die. Further, they offer possibilities for communicating with elders who, due to disabilities, may be unable to communicate in other ways.

To better understand what your parent is attempting to convey through creative expression, consider the following questions:

- Might the increased use of symbolism suggest that your parent is facing the inevitability of death?

- Is your parent revealing hidden sides of themselves that are challenging to you? Can you learn to accept these aspects as parts of human nature?

- Can you use your parent's creative expression as an avenue to deepen your contact with them?

———— COMING OF AGE PASSAGE ————
Becoming comfortable with paradox

Trashing Impression Management

In a world infatuated with image, you may be distressed as your parent becomes less invested in appearance.

The older they got, the less our parents concerned themselves with how they looked because by then they were dealing with more basic issues. When I arrived one cold winter morning to transport my father to an eye doctor appointment, he was on the front porch garbed in a silvery light blue wrap that had belonged to Mom. Chocolate rivulets outlined the folds around his mouth. I blushed, mortified. *Oh, dear. I can't take him to the clinic looking like this!*

When I handed him a tissue to wipe his face, he glared at me and retorted, "And who are we trying to impress?" To avoid a scene, I drove agreeably to the clinic, secretly hoping Dad would not draw attention to himself after arriving. But no sooner was he seated in the waiting room than he began flaunting his visual prowess by reading loudly from the local newspaper. I busied myself by working on my to-do list for the week. Luckily, his appointment went well and no one fainted when they saw him, which made me question my nagging impulse to manage his appearance.

However, soon another challenge materialized. No longer able to drive, Dad needed transportation to the community college fitness class in which John had enrolled him. Grateful for the friendships he had developed there, I agreed to be his chauffeur. During our first visit, Dad seemed confused about how to use some of the machines, but when I tried to demonstrate, he snapped that I didn't know what I was doing. I glared at him, muffled my emotions, advised, "Okay, you're on your own and I'll see you in a half hour," and stomped off to abuse a treadmill.

Within a few moments, Dad had climbed backwards onto an adjacent rowing machine and was ambitiously tugging at the "oars." Suddenly he slid to the floor, where he lay on his back dazed yet seemingly unhurt. I focused straight ahead and turned up my machine as fast as it would go to avoid reengaging his indignity, while others looked at me disapprovingly. Until I could regain my composure, it seemed better for someone else to take over.

Fortunately, two women helped Dad to his feet. Once stabilized, he padded to the locker room, where he waited while I logged in a few more miles enveloped in a curious mix of shame and self-righteousness. So engrossed was I in his projection of helplessness that I had overlooked the new accomplishment he was trying to demonstrate to me.

The ultimate challenge with Dad came during an adventure with the media. The news anchor for a local television station preparing an end-of-life feature, asked if Dad, John, and I would consent to an interview. We all agreed, and when the film crew arrived at Dad's home, he took everything in stride—sans false teeth. Pulling him aside, I whispered, "Dad, don't you want to wear your teeth for the shoot?"

"Nope," he replied. "They don't stay on very well anymore, at least not by themselves. And I hate the glue that holds them in place." I gulped, desperately wanting to accept his decision and yet embarrassed about the image he might project.

The filming proceeded and Dad was delightful, even getting in a few philosophical quips, such as, "Why is there so much fuss about what to do with a body? It's just a body."

The next evening, friends and acquaintances phoned to thank us for being so candid on the evening news. The last person to call was one of Dad's healthier peers, demanding, "How could you let your father go on TV without his teeth?" Taken aback, I told the truth. "You know, Alan, we're trying very hard as a family to respect his wishes. And sometimes that's difficult."

More and more, I could accept that physical appearance had become less of a priority for Dad. Finally, I found the shift refreshing, especially as I began to imagine my own later years. I'd smile and think, *Maybe one of the benefits of aging is transcending what others think and arriving at insights that minimize the terror of deterioration.*

If your parent's appearance begins to deteriorate . . .

If you are concerned about your parent's apparent lack of interest in physical appearance, first see if there's an underlying problem. The culprit could be mental illness, such as depression, or an incapacity akin to arthritis. Or financial constraints might be prohibiting your parent from purchasing image-boosting products or services. If none of these situations apply, and your parent's devaluation of outward appearance reflects instead a shift in values, there may be little you can do other than accept the change, support your parent's preferences, and evaluate your own priorities concerning exteriors.

To prepare for witnessing changes in your parent's style of presentation, consider the following questions:

- Are alterations in your parent's appearance related to mental or physical impairments or financial limitations, or do they signify shifting values?

- If you are uncomfortable with your parent's appearance, whose problem is it?

- Are you perhaps overinvested in impression management? Might your attempts to keep things looking tidy mask the grief you are feeling about your parent's decline?

——— COMING OF AGE PASSAGE ———
Relinquishing attachments to outward appearances

Taking Territorialism to the Streets

As your parent's control of their world slips away, territorialism may emerge.

I knew trouble was brewing when my father complained about the next-door neighbor parking in front of "the family abode." I had felt it coming. Three times earlier that week, I had pulled up to his house to find Dad's silhouette decorating the front window, letting me know he was on patrol. I tried convincing him he had no business claiming curbside territory, but he waged a full-fledged squatter's rights protest. The next day planks of wood with rows of pointed nails lined the juncture where asphalt met concrete. Scarcely avoiding the casualty of punctured tires, I made my irritation evident, causing Dad to scowl and retrieve his carpentry.

By the end of the week, Dad had invented new strategies—scattering animal excrement, deposited by passing canines, in front of the "illegally parked" cars and positioning the sprinkler alongside vehicles with open windows. At night I worried he would die a violent death at the hands of an adversary with slimy tires and drenched upholstery.

Dad's investment in protecting his parking strip was, I realized, a reaction to his increasing powerlessness in old age, and also to his vulnerability in a changed neighborhood. During the first several years he and my mother had spent in this home, the entire neighborhood had observed an unwritten code of honor. Doors were never locked; curfews were enforced; people who owned dogs cleaned up after them; individuals who borrowed tools returned them; when a neighbor was ailing, others mowed their lawn or delivered casseroles. Then a decade later, the community had been transformed, with Dad's home suddenly bordered by rentals housing a mix of college students, welfare recipients, and drug dealers. Living in what was now a high-crime area he'd become increasingly anxious about personal safety.

The coup de grâce was delivered during my visit one Sunday when a young, attractive policewoman paid a house call. Taking in her red hair, pale blue eyes, and ample curves, Dad pulled his crumpled frame up straight and feigned a polite smile before she cooed, "You know, this can't continue, Mr. G. We had another complaint—this one about windshields being waxed. You have got to stop your battle. Think of all the time and talent you've devoted to this community. You don't want to spoil it now, do you?"

"You think I soaped that guy's windshield?" Dad replied. "Hell, that's why I park my car in the garage—to avoid the vandalism around here." I refrained from interjecting that he had no car, that we had taken it from him and he had since bequeathed it to his granddaughter.

Ms. Law didn't bite. "You are the one who can stop the vandalism. In fact, we are counting on you, as someone who has made a difference on the west side of town. Will you do this for me?"

A vigilante at heart, Dad had to agree. Besides, this Kathryn Hepburn look-alike, calling on him to perform a heroic act, had made him melt.

If your parent becomes territorial . . .

If your parent has become the neighborhood's Attila the Hun, realize that behind such behavior is usually grief concerning their changed identity and circumstances. The territory your parent is protecting represents independence and security—the qualities they were accustomed to before old age traded them in for powerlessness and vulnerability.

While it is good to investigate the causes of this territorialism and keep your parent from antagonistic behavior that is dangerous or illegal, it is also necessary to realize that beyond evidence of dire risk and mental incompetence, your right to prevent your parent from engaging in turf wars is superseded by their right to make personal decisions. Attempts to control your parent are likely to prove as futile.

To better deal with your parent's overt territorialism, consider the following questions:

- Does your parent have accurate information about property rights?

- Is antagonistic behavior related to your parent's vulnerability and loss of power, or is your parent's behavior warranted? In either instance, is there a way to redirect this energy?

- Are you rewarding negative behavior and thus perpetuating it? What might be a better approach?

———— COMING OF AGE PASSAGE ————
Respecting parental boundaries

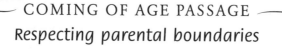

"Where Can We Rent a Metal Detector?"

If your parent has stashed items of value in the home and forgotten their location, you can interrogate, tear the house apart, or seek a less stressful option.

By the end of the 1980s, Dad's trust in the government had diminished to the point where, fearing paper money would soon be of no value, he avoided savings accounts and banks, and instead hid treasure at home. Consequently, I started receiving yearly instructions detailing sites in the family home where he had stashed his silver and gold bullion, Canadian maple leafs, African krugerrands, and ounces of platinum—most often in false-bottomed cabinets or various compartments of the upright freezer. One set of instructions was titled "Aunt Ethel's Treasure Map," Aunt Ethel being a fictitious name to maintain the secrecy of Dad's activities.

Each January, I faithfully filed the new diagram and destroyed the old one. But as Dad's memory began to fade, he started unearthing and rehiding his reserve without sending me a revised treasure map. When I questioned him about his cache, he'd simply mumble, "Yep. I've got the valuables hidden, so you'll never have to worry about anyone finding them."

When Dad died, my brothers and I attempted to locate his fortune but came up with only a few gold pieces. Dad's housekeeper, although unable to recall ever seeing his cache, did remember tossing out packages labeled "Lard" that had been in the freezer for months. Initially I considered renting a metal detector and scouring the premises for Dad's hidden treasure, but preoccupied with grief and the tasks that follow a death in the family I moved on to higher priorities. Later, when the family home was sold, I added a finders-keepers addendum to the purchase and sale agreement, stating, "All remaining contents of this residence shall become the property of the new owners . . . and may they enjoy many wonderful surprises!"

An enormous transformation in attitude had occurred the moment I gave up the quest for a metal detector. Simultaneously releasing the expectation of an inheritance, I was suddenly able to view my dad and his pitiful hoarding behavior through new eyes. I saw a man who had known tough times in which old toys, repainted to look new, were given as holiday gifts. I saw a man who had worked twelve-hour days in a box factory to attend college, who forfeited a writing career for a more secure job selling insurance to support his family, and who, according to my mother, spent sleepless nights racking his brain for strategies to pull us through financially. Respect for him followed, for despite decades of economic stress, he had paid off the house, climbed out of debt, and managed to stow cash in his wallet.

If you are expecting an inheritance from your parent . . .

Expectations of an inheritance are best released or transformed. Otherwise, given the innumerable factors that turn good intentions into unrealized dreams, you can end up with dashed hopes and bitter feelings.

To pave the way for a more authentic perspective on inheritance, consider the following questions:

- Assuming your parent is of sound mind and body, do you respect their right to manage their money as they wish?

- If money or property remains after your parent dies, do you believe you are entitled to it? On what do you base this feeling of entitlement? Can you instead learn to view your potential inheritance as a bonus?

- If your parent chooses not to bequest money to heirs but rather to spend it or give it to charity, how would you feel?

——— COMING OF AGE PASSAGE ———
Giving back to the universe

Cultivating the Kindred

Gathering with other caregivers can be not only supportive but enlightening.

In the beginning, both John and I resisted joining a caregiver's support group. We were already so consumed with our parents it seemed impossible to find time for one more activity, and we harbored the popular attitude that caring for aging parents was a family matter—a belief preventing some caregivers from asking for help until they break down. Though occasionally encountering an acquaintance in the eldercare trenches, mostly we supported each other, reaching out to siblings when overwhelmed.

John's turning point occurred when he was summoned to fetch his mother Impie, who had been banned from the Adult Day Health bus after waving her cane at fellow passengers. As the driver attempted to calm her before allowing her back on the bus, Impie interpreted her ouster as a greater challenge, poking her staff at cars and scratching their surfaces. Panicked, the driver buzzed 911 and his employer, who phoned John. It was soon after arriving at the scene that he joined an Alzheimer's support group.

Returning from his first meeting, John commented on how reassuring it was to gather with people who knew what he was going through. When he admitted to the group how disappointed he was by his mother's recovery after she had nearly died, a member said, "I know just how you feel." As others shared their stories, John realized many in this group faced more difficult challenges than he, especially a couple caring for two sets of parents, three of whom were in advanced stages of Alzheimer's.

When a few weeks later one of John's brothers confronted him with, "Mom says you're stealing her money," a group participant empathized, saying, "My dad accused me of taking his stock certificates. It turned out he couldn't remember what he'd done with them and, scared, made me the target." He added encouragingly, "John, it's pretty normal for people with dementia to get mean and insulting. Given all you are doing, attacks like this can shatter you beyond the point of being rational. Let go of the unimportant stuff and get on with the issues you need to face."

Warmed by the balm of empathy and companionship, John was able to find his center again. He began buying children's puzzles and storybooks to share with Impie, recapitulating the good times he'd had with her as a child. He also started viewing his own predicament in a more positive light, compared to the dilemmas faced by other group members, such as a divorced woman who had taken in her ex-mother-in-law because no one else would have her, and a man whose parents both had Alzheimer's.

I was less successful in finding support through a group. Instead, I reached out to close friends, many of whom were grappling with similar circumstances. When we weren't meeting for coffee in the margins of our lives, we would speak openly on the phone. I also met monthly with a staff member of a local caregiver organization, sought answers to my questions through other local and national resources, and read copiously.

If you need to reach out for support . . .

In support groups, caregivers can join as powerful allies. When our aging relatives began needing help, John and I did not understand the social service and healthcare systems for seniors and could have saved many hours of stress had we tapped into a support group sooner. Most community hospital discharge planners or disease-oriented organizations have lists of groups, including resources for people involved in the same common tasks, such as Well Spouses groups. Some of the best sources for groups are caregivers who are participating in a support forum. If support groups are not to your liking, try accessing appropriate chat rooms on the Internet or visit a library or agencies serving seniors and their families to get information about caregiving, health and disease, or community resources.

For the best help, select a support group carefully. Before joining one, visit several, if possible, to find the most personally appealing style of facilitation. The ideal moderator is an individual who has had caregiving experience, possesses good facilitation skills, is not afraid of emotions, and is available between sessions. The ideal group is one that expresses empathy, compassion, and honesty; willingly offers strategies, feedback, and encouragement; and confronts members who resist moving from victimization toward gratitude for their eldercare experience.

To help face the possibility of finding an eldercare support group, consider the following questions:

- Are you opposed to joining a support group or meeting regularly and informally with others involved in eldercare? What might make you more receptive to these ideas?

- What wisdom, experience, or skills could you bring to a support group?

- What activity are you willing to sacrifice in order to take advantage of a support group?

——— COMING OF AGE PASSAGE ———
Actively seeking help when necessary

Birthday Wish to Die

You may not be ready to let go of your parent even when they welcome the end of their life.

On his ninetieth birthday, my father mused, "Why am I still living?" His tone was serious; the flock of party-goers hushed up.

Recovering from shock, I quipped, "Because we need you, Dad!"

"You're number's not up yet, Pop," jibed my brother Kip. "You've got at least another decade to go!"

Finally, son-in-law Bill rescued the festive ambiance with, "You're just too darn ornery, Papa," sending even Dad into gales of laughter. Then the doorbell rang and in twirled a male ballerina in a tutu, loaded with balloons and a personalized song for my father. Dad rolled his eyes but knew this was his just due for all the years he had played practical jokes on family members. Reviving his stage presence, Dad hammed it up with the performer, stretching his elastic face into expressions of surprise, mock anger, and good humor for the ten minutes the actor had been hired to perform.

As the actor left, Dad looked perplexed, finally asking, "Who the heck was that? Did I ever play a joke on him?" Then the faraway look in his eyes returned.

In the weeks following, Dad dwelled on why he was still alive, often when least expected—such as midway into a favorite story or a doze. The phrase always startled me. *Has life lost its purpose? Is he bored?* I wondered.

While he used to dash off lively letters to the editor of the local newspaper, now his typing was nearly impossible to decipher and he got agitated if I offered to take dictation for him. Moreover, few of Dad's friends called anymore, and when they did he strained to hear them and sometimes to remember their names and faces. Those who dropped by unannounced were greeted randomly with a sunny smile or a dark frown, depending on Dad's internal weather system.

Subsequently, I too began wondering why he was still alive, aware that he had been slowly disengaging himself from a life of *doing* while thrust into the foreign soil of *being*. I attempted to help him overcome his despondency by bringing notebooks in which he could record his philosophy concerning countless topics, an activity with which he grudgingly cooperated for a while. In addition, we took drives around the community to look at locations connected to his past life, such as the school he had attended and his childhood home. Relying on the address book he could no longer read, I prepared labels for him to use in writing letters to friends and family but later found the labels in the trash. Though I had read about death and dying, it was agonizing to see there was nothing I could do to change his course. His focus was beginning to shift past his family, friends, and the tiny corner of worldly space he inhabited.

Finally, I knew Dad was well into a journey from which I could not rescue him and that it was time for me to surrender. This realization was triggered, in part, by the memory of a deceased neighbor who at age ninety-seven began asking the same question as Dad: "Why am I still living?" When I protested, she confessed that she had tried to talk to her family about her wish to die but they would not hear of it. As I learned to acknowledge her words, she felt comfortable expressing her despair. Later she thanked me for accepting her feelings without judgment.

Now I wondered if I could just accept my father's wish to die rather than attempting to rob him of it. At first I felt compelled to distract him from his pain. But gradually, through listening, I discovered the value of just being with him—breathing in my love and breathing out my grief.

It was soon clear my job was to stay out of his way and celebrate the moments he touched bases with me. Apparently, as we are in birth we are in death—flung on our own toward an unknown destination.

If your parent's connection to life is fading . . .

If your parent expresses a desire to die, think seriously about joining a support group of other caregivers. Alternatively, find someone with whom you can share your experience of grief and of frustration at your inability to interest your parent in life. To prepare for this stage in caregiving, consider the following questions:

- How might you become a safety net for a parent who no longer wishes to live?

- Are you able to let go of your own concerns fully enough to respect your parent's reality?

- Do you know where to find support for your lack of power to change the situation?

——— COMING OF AGE PASSAGE ———

Being present for your parent as you grieve

From Civil Disobedience to Assisted Living

Some transitions are for going through—*rather than* around.

Learning from a neighbor that my father had turned into a "creature of the night," roaming the streets after midnight and prowling throughout his three stories before dawn, we reluctantly realized he had crossed the line from risky to dangerous by remaining in his own home. So when my brother Ed came to visit he offered to introduce Dad to a few assisted living facilities.

Their first destination was Just-Like-Home Assisted Living. Predicting Dad would sabotage the mission if forewarned, Ed offered him a "cruise in the countryside." As the car hummed over gently rolling hills, Dad's eyelids grew heavy and he lapsed into a midmorning snooze. But as Ed swerved into Just-Like-Home's circular driveway, Dad awoke with a start, splaying his body across the passenger seat and whimpering, "No, no, no . . ."

Concerned that Dad might have a heart attack, Ed squawked, "It's okay, Dad. We'll go home now." It was the last of their assisted living expeditions.

A few months later, a neighbor called to report that my high-maintenance father had been pacing the street at night pleading for a cribbage partner but unable to remember his quests in the morning. Immediately John and I searched for a facility that could offer Dad emotional support. However, after three days of previewing adult family homes and assisted living facilities, we had to concede that most residents were too mentally or physically challenged to offer companionship to a man who hungered for intellectual debates. We also supposed that Dad's flips from Mr. Convivial to Master Hermit might raise suspicions that he was delusional.

Fortunately we discovered the Shangri-la of long-term care, a facility that was only two blocks away, affordable, and run by an owner-manager who demonstrated impeccable social skills with elders. Gently approaching Dad, we explained, "We're nearing the time to find a place where you can get a little more help than we can offer. We can choose a spot on our own or you can check them out with us. What do you think?" At this point, he knew he was beat and begrudgingly agreed to preview the home the next day.

But when we came to pick him up, Dad was dressed for rejection, looking like a tramp in frayed sleeves and mildewed tennis shoes he'd retrieved from the garden shed. Nevertheless, we ushered him into the car and cranked up the radio to drown out last-minute protests during the seven-minute drive to the home.

As soon as he stepped inside, Dad prepared to project a bad impression. A dark-eyed staff member greeted us and led Dad to an overstuffed chair. Recalling the information supplied on the application form I had completed earlier, she said, "Cart, we understand you are a golf lover and you enjoy sending letters to the editor of the newspaper. What other things do you like to do?"

Dad paused, theatrically galvanizing everyone's full attention, then announced, "Well, I like to break furniture."

The staff member's smile faded, yet she bounced back. "I noticed you petting the dog when you came in. Do you like cats too? We're going to be getting a cat soon."

On stage again, Dad arched an eyebrow and pulled the corners of his mouth in opposite directions. "Yes," he drawled at last. "I like to hang them from their hind legs and extract their claws—one by one."

The attendant rose and said to John and me, "Why don't you leave Cart with us and come back in about a half hour."

Miraculously, by the time we returned, Dad was gazing charmingly into the eyes of a woman who appeared to be his new soul mate and patting the attendant's hand. On our way to the car a few minutes later, Dad quipped, "Yes, this *is* a fine place. And do you know I met a woman who used to play bridge with your mother? They say they will have a room ready for me in two weeks." Everything seemed to be going as we had hoped.

However, five days before he was to vacate his home, Dad relapsed into rebellion with a series of nocturnal episodes, falling out of his recliner and turning over furniture in an attempt to lift himself from the floor, coating the linoleum with gigantic spills of juice, and bedding himself on the kitchen counter at night. So John and I took turns spending the night with him.

On the morning of moving day, John left Dad's house, and allowing for a fifteen-minute changing of the guard, I headed over. Opening the front door, I heard a heavy thud and saw Dad facedown on the floor bleeding from his nose. Lifting his head, he mumbled, "All right, all right. I'll go." I applied Band-Aids to his cut and helped him get dressed. For the return trip to Shangri-la he chose a freshly pressed shirt, Docker slacks, and polished loafers, showing a marked transition away from shabby un-chic.

By comparison, Dad's ultimate relocation was stressful. The forfeiture of his home evoked anguish at the loss of precious memories–not only for Dad, who seemed unusually receptive to hugging, but for the entire family.

If your parent is adamant about living at home . . .

Some parents anticipate the need for a housing change in their later years and willingly plan ahead; many don't but will agree to new quarters; others, like my father, will dig in their heels and refuse to cooperate until some catastrophe exacts a surrender. Talks about safety, while effective for some parents, did not work with Dad. He preferred to spend his later life in the home he had known, surmising he would die there suddenly from a heart attack or stroke. No amount of reasoning could steer him toward a more prudent position before his intervening crisis.

The events surrounding moving day for a recalcitrant elder cannot help but engender pain, yet such agony can be strengthening because it encourages mature responses that balance intuition with logic. Previously, these faculties may have been in conflict, with intuition having you promise never to move your parent and logic insisting on relocation. Now, you may have to change your position and apologize for your earlier, naive pledge. In general, any time your parent asks for a guarantee against relocation, the most balanced reply is, "I can only take the best actions possible based on my knowledge at any given time."

To prepare for the possibility of having to relocate a parent, explore the following questions:

- Is your elderly parent at risk by staying in their home? Is your parent receptive to an assessment of their capacity to live independently?

- Have you previewed assisted living options? Are there more facilities you might visit?

- Have you practiced allowing intuition and logic to work together? What adjustments might be required?

- If relocation becomes necessary, how will you honor your own losses and your parent's?

—— COMING OF AGE PASSAGE ——
Surviving tough decisions

PART 4

Family Affairs

Invariably, a family's unfinished business will surface during eldercare. Families are vulnerable to changing dynamics any time divergent values, unresolved conflicts, and geographical separations interface. And in times of eldercare, when rapport with siblings or other significant relatives may be easily disrupted, emotions can explode, causing all parties to feel desperate, powerless, or unappreciated. Often this prompts the formation of alliances through negative childhood patterns, especially passive-aggressive behaviors that may have worked in the past but are now counterproductive.

The challenge in facing unfinished business is to rise to the greater good—fulfilling the wishes of parents, making sure they feel safe and protected, and "walking with" them in their final years. Being unfamiliar with this role, we may at times need to solicit the support of more objective individuals to avoid complications.

When John and I became caregivers for our parents, it was like we had been playing tag and were chosen as "it"! With our lives suddenly complicated by caregiving responsibilities, we envied our siblings' relatively normal existences. On bad days, the siren Resentment seduced us and we'd complain about our fate.

Did we ever say, "It's not fair!" or think about evading our responsibilities? Absolutely. Were we prepared for the spilling of secrets as family interaction increased? Hardly. Did we respond graciously when a relative offered professional medical advice without being asked? No. Did we expect to be thanked profusely by family members and suffer disappointment when we weren't? Yes. Were we hurt to find our unified vision illusory because everyone had a path of their own? Without a doubt. But did we ultimately strive for unity in eldercare and feel rewarded by growing personally? Yes indeed.

As your own family sets forth on the arduous road of caring for parents, simple measures can preserve the felt sense of unity. One is a family meeting held either in person or by conference call. The purpose of this meeting is to form a network of support by expressing expectations, evaluating assumptions, and clarifying roles.

A second strategy for sustaining family oneness is an agreement to stay in touch and communicative. In an ideal world, the family's job is to back up the primary caregiver so they can focus on assisting the ailing parent. However in our culture, where extensive help is rarely offered unless solicited, roles and responsibilities may have to be constantly revised, and permission granted to speak up specifically about any needs that arise. Key caregivers must be permitted to ask for emotional support, just as family members who feel isolated by distance or excluded should be encouraged to express their remorse.

Also, prioritize the caregiving above all, even if this means giving up control at times or participating in unforeseen ways. If you are the primary caregiver preparing for a week of respite, and a sibling flies in and begins micromanaging the hired help or purchasing prepared meals for your parent, let your sibling take charge. Or if you want to help but are reticent about parental contact, consider contributing financially so the primary caregiver can hire assistance and take a breather.

The most critical element to include in any blueprint for preserving family unity at this time is teamwork. Siblings and others who collaborate not only surmount the most difficult challenges posed by caregiving but also transform old vendettas into more promising family affairs. The give-and-take of cooperation ensures optimal care for your parent and also a sense that after they are gone the rest of the family will live on free of regrets about this time of transition.

Responsibility Roulette

Unless you are an only child, topflight eldercare hinges on cultivating a team approach with your siblings rather than relying on random responsibility.

When our parents simultaneously began to fail, our siblings pledged support and we all shelved prior relationship difficulties. We circled the wagons, believing in Roslyn Carter's concept that "caregiving is not an endeavor that should be done alone." However, although blood, loyalty, and mutual affection bound us together in the first months of caregiving, old patterns soon emerged, making us feel we had to work at creating a more collaborative arrangement so we could address the different aspects of caring for our parents.

In coming to terms with these realities as caregivers, we faced the following issues:

Geography. It was self-evident that John and I, the sole family members living in the same vicinity as our parents, would serve as primary caregivers and our siblings, all brothers, would support us from afar.

Extended family. Each sibling had married, bringing spouses and added responsibilities to the mix. Of the six couples, two had children to raise and another had a second set of aging parents to care for.

Careers. John and I had more flexibility in our schedules than our siblings, whose jobs required their full-time presence.

Money. While John and I could donate our time, some of our siblings were able to chip in for things our parents' budgets could not cover such as lawn care. Others were not in a position to contribute financially and even found it expensive to visit.

Personality. Some family members skillfully blended *doing* with *being,* by combining chores with meaningful social contact,

FAMILY AFFAIRS ———— 141

such as my sister-in-law Kelly, who mailed greeting cards or cookies to Dad when she and her husband weren't able to visit. Others had difficulty dealing with the idea of parental illness or death.

Interactions. Midway into eldercare, I decided to address communication frustrations with my brothers. When they called and asked how I was doing and I began reciting a perplexing event, they tended to offer advice, a response I perceived as a spin-off of the problem-solving expertise required in their careers. What I needed, and finally told them, was not guidance but just someone to listen and understand.

Professional skills. Because of our careers in education and management consultation, John and I may have had more knowledge about interpersonal dynamics than our siblings. Even so, until we acknowledged the emotional undertow at work in our respective families, our progress was marginal. Consequently, we do not advise professionals in any supportive capacity—law, finance, medicine, health care, or psychology—to act as experts for the family.

Philosophies. Diverse religious, spiritual, and political ideologies thrived among our siblings. Fortunately, we agreed on the common goal of honoring our parents' wishes, though we sometimes had to struggle with the means for achieving it.

Expression of feelings. Without honest and ongoing communication, siblings may miss opportunities for cooperation and understanding. Primary caregivers need to remember that siblings uninvolved in the day-to-day care of a parent often have strong feelings about both their parent and their own level of involvement in caregiving. If critical decisions are made without their input, resentments can flare. Similarly, absent siblings have a responsibility to stay in touch and collaborate long distance. Those who do, struggle less with assessing which crises require visits involving transportation costs and arrangements, leaves from job responsibilities, and time away from spouse and family. Communicating honestly in such circumstances may require expressing one's heartrending concern about not being able to arrive in time for the last good-bye to a dying parent.

If family members are about to decide on their roles in eldercare . . .

You may have a family that works together fluidly without major conflict. Or your kin might be so accustomed to crisis because of an alcoholic father or a chronically ill mother that informal caregiving roles are already in place. Even in these instances it is wise to remember that unexpressed assumptions discussed early in the planning stages of eldercare can help prevent conflict later.

In our situation, all siblings imagined the stint would be short since our parents appeared to be rapidly declining. But the farther it continued beyond our expectations, the more we seemed to disagree on how best to proceed. The source of our contradictions eventually became clear: having ignored earlier signs of our parents' deterioration, we had been exaggerating their symptoms, making a quantum leap to the idea that their lives would end shortly and we therefore faced a state of great urgency. With this understanding we were able to reassess the circumstances and transform our approach.

To guard against conflicts with family members while caregiving a parent, consider in advance the following questions:

- How well do you really know your siblings—physically, emotionally, mentally, and spiritually? If your knowledge is limited, what measures might you take to enhance it? Can you participate in activities together instead of merely conversing?

- What individual sensitivities do you need to keep in mind when negotiating the duties of caregiving?

- What eldercare role is best suited to each family member? Are the roles similar to those played in your family of origin? Should they be renegotiated?

- What family communication skills need to be refined?
- Will you and your siblings engage in periodic family meetings? Who will conduct these meetings? (For information about family meetings, see Appendix B, pages 227–232.)
- If some meetings will require third-party facilitation, where can you find a good mediator?

——— COMING OF AGE PASSAGE ———
Valuing cooperation as a common goal

The Birth-Order Boogie

Now that your parents have entered the deep forest of old age, family conflicts resulting from birth order may provide new opportunities for healing.

Our parents' decline into the thicket of senior citizenry and our new roles as their primary caregivers together formed a springboard for examining the implications of birth order in our families and how it pertained to competition among siblings. I was a firstborn, while John was the middle child. Early on, I decided that being cooperative would earn me my parents' esteem. Like many eldest children, I intuited the "rules" and was on constant alert to avoid causing trouble. For example, having bypassed crawling I walked at age one, and by fourteen months I was toilet trained.

My brother Kip's arrival pushed me out of the spotlight I'd enjoyed for three years. Struggling to regain my former status, I cultivated an industriousness that made me an overachiever with an exaggerated sense of responsibility. Kip, meanwhile, was physical—swimming at age two and, like "true boys" of the time, fond of playing cowboys and collecting rocks, insects, and baseball cards. Despite my determination to surpass him, I was outwitted one afternoon while entertaining friends of my parents with songs I'd recently learned at Bible school. Kip bolted into the room cloaked only in a blanket, flipped it open briefly, and announced, "Ha, ha. You can't see my penis." An incorrigible prankster, Kip struggled academically until I left for college, though today he has a Ph.D.

The arrival of second brother Ed, eleven years after my birth, posed a problem of an odd man out. Kip and I competed for Ed's attention, and the winner was rewarded with entertainment springing spontaneously from our baby brother's razor-edged mind and sense of humor.

The sibling relationships in John's family were different. His older brother Charles, an introvert, was a National Merit finalist and an accomplished pianist, while John was interested in sports and country and western music. Joe, the youngest brother, valued spontaneity and amused the family with his wit. Alliances were obvious. Charles aligned with Mom, considering himself responsible for taking care of both her and his younger brothers; Joe connected more with Dad; and John felt the need to escort Charles into social situations and to facilitate Joe's rite of passage into adolescence.

John's patterns and mine occasionally emerged as our parents' health began to fail. When John's older brother criticized him for decisions he was making about Impie, John would immediately fantasize physically overpowering Charles as he had in junior high school. My routine, as the oldest sibling, was to make myself continually available to my parents, trading sleep for promises when necessary. To harness my need for control and access to them, I marked my territory in many ways, such as suggesting things my brothers could do rather than letting them arrive at their own conclusions. Despite our best efforts to understand these regressive compensating behaviors, we were caught between primitive reactions and adult responses, lapsing too often into refusal to acknowledge our parents' deterioration. Until we were willing to break through denial, our transitions were not authentic.

If you have siblings and are unaware of the behavioral implications of birth order...

Since the family is the basis for all later relationships in life, understanding your sibling relationships can help you interpret not only how you relate to friends and colleagues but numerous family dynamics during the time of caregiving. It is therefore an especially good idea to reflect on the part you played in early sibling interactions.

To prepare for birth-order improvisations, consider the following questions:

- In what ways were you valued by your parents? Can you identify any roles you assumed that correlate with this perception?

- With whom outside the family have you practiced these behaviors? Is your identity at work similar to that in the family?

- If you and your siblings were competitive, how did each of you express these rivalries?

- How might a reemergence of these behaviors affect your eldercare experience? What strengths might you instead draw from early family life?

———— COMING OF AGE PASSAGE ————

Understanding the legacy of family dynamics

The Fairness Factor

Expecting life to be measured by a yardstick of fairness may leave you disappointed.

As primary caregivers, John and I secretly kept score on our fairness tally, registering our involvement in comparison with that of siblings and other relatives. When we incurred financial losses, forfeited career opportunities or air tickets, or postponed an evening out because we couldn't find in-home support for our parents, we would sometimes feel other family members were not shouldering enough responsibility for eldercare.

But such discrepancies were minor in relation to several apparent injustices, all emotionally charged. The first such incident occurred when my mom muttered that of her three children only one had never been difficult. Another happened when John's brother Joe came to visit Impie, and John, who had done the "heavy lifting" for ten years, left momentarily to meet with the hospice chaplain, whereupon Impie died in Joe's arms.

A third seemingly unjust event unfolded after John had spent hours writing a contract to clarify the roles of Impie's in-home caregivers, only to have it criticized by a relative. Included in the document was the suggestion that employees who receive conflicting messages from the family about Impie's care ask John, as primarily caregiver, to resolve the disagreement. When the contract went into effect, the relative took John to task about his assumption of authority—a critique John felt was unfair. He conceded, however, that a better solution would have been to let everyone review the contract before it was implemented.

I also felt injustice at times, especially when out-of-town family came to visit my father and the depressed demeanor he had shared with me as the "safe" family member would suddenly lift, revealing his underlying charm and vitality. After many such incidents, a good friend helped me gain perspective, saying, "Gail, why are you so focused on fairness? When have things ever been fair in life?"

It took numerous derailed expectations for John and I to finally figure out that fairness was a myth. We saw that the sooner we let our slights and offenses take center stage, the more the gifts of eldercare awaiting us remained veiled. Ultimately we discovered that primary caregiving was not about fairness at all but about rewards from participation, which far outweighed the sacrifices. Among the most significant rewards were opportunities for a deepening intimacy with our parents, compassion toward others, and faith. We also came to better understand boundaries, the importance of asking for help, and transitions from aging to dying to death. We improved our crisis skills as well, able eventually to retain balance and even a sense of humor during events that otherwise might have been interpreted as catastrophic. While closing the last chapters on eldercare, we had the satisfaction that our whole family had done the best it could to maintain everyone's health, emotional fulfillment, and dignity.

If you begin obsessing about fairness . . .

If you are just starting out in eldercare, you may not see the immediate returns, but if you take care of yourself as you embrace the adventure, there will be many wonderful benefits. It is advantageous to keep this perspective in mind when injustices seem to occur regarding your role in eldercare.

To prepare for dealing with the realities of unfairness, consider the following questions:

- How often do you think about fairness in relation to your caregiving activities and the roles of other family members? What feelings do you have about the concept of fairness in life?

- Are you aware that gifts await you in eldercare? What do you imagine they might be in your situation?

• Along with challenges, can you treasure having time with your parent? What mutual gains might there be in this relationship?

———— COMING OF AGE PASSAGE ————
Leaving Never-Never Land

Caregiver Currency

The primary caregiver decision is one of the more revealing events of eldercare.

At one stage in caregiving I experienced burnout, and although I wanted to blame others for my state, upon reflection I had to conclude I was the one largely responsible for it. I noticed, for example, that if someone counseled me on ways to lighten my load, saying, "You know, your dad could probably be doing some of the tasks you're doing for him" or "Why don't you share more of your caregiving tasks with others?" I was quick to rationalize my take-charge behavior.

Yet at the same time, I began to increasingly resent sacrifices I made in the course of caregiving. For instance, one time when we had arranged to attend my sister-in-law's retirement party in Portland, the evening before our departure Dad had a temperature of 102 degrees and chills. So John and I agreed it would be best for him to make the excursion solo and for me to stay home with Dad. After John left, my worries gave way to resentment: my family was off together celebrating while I was left alone with Dad.

Soon it was determined that Dad had a sinus infection, and after prescribing an antibiotic the doctor suggested I hire a home care professional, get on a plane the next morning, and forget Dad for forty-eight hours—advice I gladly accepted. Arriving in time for the retirement dinner, I shifted into a celebratory mode, happy for the change of scene. The next morning the women shopped while the men played golf, then we all met for dinner at a Thai restaurant. But despite the jovial atmosphere at dinner, I began descending toward a nervous breakdown and told John I needed to leave. A relative noticed us preparing to depart and, offended that we were breaking up the festivity, asked, "What's the matter with Gail?"

Overhearing his comment, I retorted, "If you have an issue with me, talk to me directly."

Then my angry relative demanded, "What the hell is wrong with you?" Suddenly, the two of us were like three year olds screaming at each other across a table while the rest of our entourage scurried out the door and into a nearby restaurant for dessert.

Though our follow-up exchange led to tears on both our parts and a deeper connection, I knew the jig was up: I was clearly burned out from excessive caregiving. I had to reflect on my motivations for becoming a primary caregiver and find new ways to deal with eldercare. In doing this, I discovered that as the oldest child in our family and a female, I had always been more comfortable giving than receiving, a behavior referred to as "codependency." The job description I'd written for myself as a child had been to take care of others, especially my dad, and I expected a payoff for my efforts: his love. Now, as his primary caregiver, I was still making a play for Dad's love and my family's appreciation, unaware of the currency I was stockpiling by pleasing him, often at my own expense.

If you are suffering burnout from caregiving . . .

If you decide to shoulder your parent's care, understand that this choice is on a par with the decision to marry or have a child, and it will have long-range effects on the lives of everyone in your household. Because your time and freedom will be significantly restricted by eldercare, it's best to make this decision only after deliberating long and hard. Plumb your past history to examine your motives and if they are likely to bear fruit or need to be changed.

Whatever your analysis, if you are burned out, angry, or resentful, you have waited too long to ask for help. The solution is to let go and get support, even if the relief helpers do not do things the way you'd like. Though your stockpile may forfeit a deposit or two, without this sacrifice you might lose your health.

To determine your motivations for becoming a primary caregiver and whether you are at risk for caregiver burnout, consider the following questions:

- Are you better at caring for others than yourself?

- Do you see this role as an opportunity to gain a position of esteem in your family or a "second chance" to gain approval from your mother, father, or other family members or peers?

- Is your commitment to caregiving a way to "do the right thing"?

- Are you falling into a pattern of caring too much? If so, can you take a break or get relief help?

- Have you taken over some of your parent's self-care functions?

- Do you recognize that caring too much is not really caring since if you burn out you are no good to yourself or others?

- Are you sharing eldercare with other family members? Could you distribute responsibilities more equitably among them?

——— COMING OF AGE ———
Taking an honest look at what drives your caring

When "I Will" Means "I Won't"

Interpreting indirect communication is a tall order, unless you are willing to take off your blinders and see the compliance camouflage at work.

Both John and I recognized the I-will-but-I-won't game from years before because we had played it with each other. Never publicly acknowledging our bargaining tactics, we had acted instinctively, reasoning as follows:

> John: *If I say "yes" to a request you make, I will please you.*
>
> Gail: *If I say "yes" to a request you make, then I establish myself as a responsive partner and can accrue more bargaining power.*

Despite our best intentions, when John didn't follow through on his commitments, I would get angry, a response he did not understand because he felt he had done his job by saying "yes." When I made a commitment, I would follow through regardless of the cost, but if my commitment was insincere I would get furious at myself and transfer my anger to John.

When it became obvious this convoluted modus operandi was not working for us, we got help and stopped making agreements we knew we would break or resent, offering each other feedback to facilitate personal reality checks. I learned to say to John, "I don't believe you," while he would proffer, "Are you doing this because you think you should or because you want to?"

These new insights into negotiation proved invaluable in elder-care situations involving siblings and other relatives. About 80 percent of the time eldercare commitments were honored, although occasionally someone would drop the ball, leaving us on our own to ignore or tackle a difficult dilemma. For example, a brother who had agreed to handle the accounting for a parent's money suddenly abandoned the task because we would not fire a helper he believed had filched one of the family tablecloths. Due to our increased awareness of the psychological tricks played in negotiating, we were able to better interpret the message behind his behavior: "I'll help if you do it my way."

Another time, a relative agreed to deliver bad news to a parent but later decided he could not do it after all. His unspoken message translated differently: "I can't handle their anger or disappointment. Besides, confrontations are your job, not mine."

Since John and I frequently felt drained and vulnerable, when family members failed to follow through with an eldercare agreement we often gave up prematurely rather than pressing the issue. However, over time we learned not to take people's lack of follow-through quite so personally. Frequently we had to remind ourselves, "Rights and wrongs don't matter in the long run. All we can do is learn from the messes and work on ourselves."

If you or others in the family are not fulfilling eldercare commitments . . .

When family members send mixed messages regarding their responsibilities or renege on an agreement, most primary caretakers are confused but give them the benefit of the doubt. At times primary caretakers may question their own communication skills or make excuses for relatives, such as the following:

"Perhaps she didn't understand, so I'll give her another chance."

"She's been so busy, she probably just forgot."

"I should not have asked him. He's got so much going on in his personal life."

Another common response is to get mad and, not wanting to incite a family feud, protest indirectly by becoming uncooperative, sabotaging the promise breaker, or withdrawing. Reminding a relative about a commitment they have made is also an option, but it may leave you eventually taking over the responsibility to a chorus of personalized excuses like "Well, why didn't you remind me again?" or "You know I'm a procrastinator. Why can't you just accept that?"

Unfulfilled commitments prompt diverse justifications. Some may be legitimate, such as illness or the necessity of suddenly having to leave town. Others may relay indirect messages, such as claims about the unfair sharing of a burden or rebellion against taking orders. Still others may reveal an initial consent for purposes of pleasing but no intention to follow through. Primary caregivers benefit from seeking more information so they can interpret broken agreements and turn bargaining tactics and other rationalizations into hands-on assistance in eldercare.

If your family is more comfortable communicating directly, it may cause conflict, but ultimately it will promote better understanding and cooperation. As you negotiate for full family participation in an aging parent's care, be aware of the dynamics surrounding commitments of support, then determine the changes that may need to be made. In the event you find some members making empty promises, consider the following questions:

- Are your requests of family members adequately specific? Do you confirm their understandings of requests?

- Do you forgive or minimize others' inability to honor commitments by making excuses for them?

- Do you recognize and understand your family's history of conflict, including the dynamics that resulted in successful outcomes?

- Are you a model for saying "no" when necessary? If not, are you willing to develop this ability?

———— COMING OF AGE PASSAGE ————
Relinquishing blind trust and naïveté

"Mom Always Did Like You Best!"

Worrying about favoritism can keep you stuck in the purgatory of sibling rivalry, unable to surrender to universal issues.

One time when my mother was in the intensive care unit, I could not engage her in eye contact. At first I wrote it off as an effect of her stroke, but as I watched my brother arrive at her bedside and Mom gaze lovingly into his eyes, my radar blared. This situation made me feel that I was once again a needy child except now the stakes were higher. I worried that opportunities for receiving Mom's love might slip away.

After both my parents had died, Mom's childhood friend Lenora and I made a point of getting together every couple of months. Hungry for more stories about Mom and treasuring Lenora's wisdom, I coveted our contact. Not only did her point of view enhance understanding of my family, it opened doors for growth. On one occasion, I observed, "Since mothers and fathers love each child in different ways, it's easy for kids to interpret one or another of these expressions as favoritism."

"That's true," said Lenora. "In your family, though, Kip was the favorite with your dad."

Stunned, I muttered, "Well, I knew he was the one Mom preferred, but I didn't know that about Dad." I thought to myself, *Surely I was Dad's favorite, wasn't I?*

Later in the day, I shared Lenora's comment with John, who disagreed with her perception, stating, "That's just one person's opinion, Gail. You and your dad had a terrific relationship."

I protested, "That's not the point. It's that I always thought I was the most special to Dad." The secret I had harbored throughout my lifetime was out of the bag.

Over the next week, I reacted to Lenora's statement in stages. First, I indulged in jealousy and wrestled with self-worth. Next, I was furious, thinking, *After all the hard work I've done competing for attention, how dare the family not reward me with some sign of favoritism.* Finally, I laughed, having escaped at last from the self-made prison sentence. No longer did I have to be wonderful to gain affection from my parents—or the corps of replicas to whom I had transferred authority throughout the years, such as my teachers and employers. I thought with relief, *If I never accomplish another thing in life, I'll still be good enough.*

After reflection, I realized that my need to feel special was chronic and that Dad had been my major target. No doubt this fixation influenced my willingness to be his primary caregiver, although I believe the decision was also motivated by genuine compassion.

Gradually I was able to accept my contentiousness as normal and develop empathy for myself struggling so hard to be worthy of love. As more time passed, my siblings and I began to share our personal experiences with rivalry, thus gaining a better understanding of our family dynamics.

If you are experiencing sibling rivalry during caregiving . . .

If sibling rivalry rears its head during parental caregiving, try to gain perspective on the situation. Remember that in a competitive society there is too much emphasis on scarcity issues rather than seeing the world as an abundant source of love for everyone. In addition, it is helpful to compare the sibling rivalry of adults with the sibling rivalry experienced in childhood to better understand how you may have grown or how your family dynamics may have changed because of eldercare.

To gain perspective on sibling rivalry you might experience during eldercare, consider the following questions:

• From your perspective, if either of your parents had a favorite child who was it? Do others share your perception? What meaning do you attach to your conclusion and how did you compete?

- How was sibling rivalry addressed in your family?
- Which childhood experiences can your siblings help you better understand?
- How has eldercare changed sibling rivalry in your family?

———— COMING OF AGE PASSAGE ————
Facing what you feared most

Reorganizing the Family Skeleton Closet

Whether for confessional or informational purposes, your parent tells you stories, some of which might change your image of them, the family, or even yourself.

Most families selectively hide or withhold truths about themselves, hoping to minimize pain, abandonment, or shame for their members. But if the saying "You're as sick as your secrets" is accurate, honesty can be cathartic for current and future generations.

As a child, I sensed that if my family completed their sentences surely I would have a great American novel, but no matter how hard I pressed my ear to a vent or balanced like a gargoyle atop the wide fireplace mantel, I caught only snatches of dialogue. At family gatherings, scotch or Dad's home brew did sometimes loosen the starch—like when one of my aunts could no longer wait to use the toilet and peed in a wastebasket, or when two uncles gave my five-year-old brother a Mohawk haircut, each shaving one side of his head. However, an invisible barrier always separated the topics suitable for children from those discussed by adults. I suspected undisclosed family history whenever my father exchanged glances with my uncle, or Mom guided her sister-in-law to another room for fear they would say too much.

Certain past and present events remained unmentionable elephants in the room—until my great-aunt, Ms. Leaky Valve, broke the silence. Too old and worn down to keep protecting the family secrets, she finally divulged the darkest truths, both awful and wonderful. The more Ms. Leaky Valve went public, the more my parents looked the other way, never elaborating or indulging in emotional release. As in many families, when mine began to reveal its dark side, unrecorded suicides, addictions, miscarriages and infant deaths, incest, previous marriages, affairs, homosexuality, arson, and blackmail were among the revelations. Though some relatives refused to believe certain incidents, preferring to remain in denial, most learned through hindsight and forged ahead, splicing the repercussions of unfortunate choices.

To date, I have never understood how my parents' generation could have withheld so many secrets without exploding. Perhaps they were intent on avoiding anguish, respecting privacy, or remaining positive. Or maybe they simply accepted the darkness within the light, like the movie star who when asked how he had managed to adapt to a debilitating disease replied, "Well, this is my life!"

If your aging parent or other relatives expose family secrets . . .

During the period you spend caring for a parent, many family secrets may be unleashed, in part because emergencies and endings evoke intimacy. Your parent might wish to share previously hidden life details in your presence; or a disgruntled in-law may reveal unknown segments of your mother's or father's past. Although each disclosure may challenge your image of the family and your heritage, it will also create a pathway for family catharsis and personal growth.

To prepare for the possible revelation of long-held family secrets emerging like skeletons from an ancient closet, consider the following questions:

- What are your family norms with respect to honesty and disclosure? Do the benefits of divulging family secrets seem to outweigh the risks and appear timely?
- How willing are you to assume the role of "bad guy" if you perceive that revealing the past will enhance family communication, healing, and growth?
- If you yourself have kept family secrets, are you clear about your intentions for sharing this information?
- How would the revelation of a dark side of your family affect your perception of family members and feelings about your heritage?

——— COMING OF AGE PASSAGE ———
Inviting family secrets into visibility

Sidelining Mother-in-Law Syndrome

It is never too late to change the film in your internal camera.

Like many daughters, my tie with my parents was stronger than it was with my in-laws. Four years into our marriage I was still adjusting to the cultural milieu of my new family, preferring the familiarity of my own. Unconsciously, I saw to it my parents were more favored in our new home, displaying more photographs of them than of John's family. For the most part, John fell into line with this practice, having felt more connected outside his family circle.

It was not that my in-laws were unloving, unaccepting, or ungenerous toward me, only that they were *different*. I had not foreseen that John and I each inherited traits for which we had not bargained, and at first we interpreted our dissimilarities as potentially threatening.

Enter a grandchild, Greg, the spitting image of his father; factor in my excessive lack of confidence around new babies, demonstrated by a decision to stop breastfeeding three weeks into Greg's life; underscore my mother-in-law Impie's propensity to claim only Goeller-credit for this baby replica of John and her recitals about what I *should* do with a new baby; and splice in my immaturity. The result was combustion, and eventually ossification following a couple of decades of "lock-in."

Fueled by Impie's criticisms, I felt like a failure as a new mom—a Wicked Witch of the North, short-tempered, depressed, and overwhelmed as John took the family car to work each day, or attended graduate school and refereed sports in the scant margins of his life.

But that began to change when we had school-age children who didn't need their parents or grandparents in the same ways. We fell asleep for a moment and our kids were in high school preparing for college. And by the time our parents were aging, no one was more surprised than I to feel my attitude toward my mother-in-law soften.

One day, Impie and I were alone in our home. Spotting some correspondence bearing her name on John's desk, she shouted, "You are stealing my mail," and turned on me, her cane poised for attack. I tried to reassure her but, angry and scared, I thought, *She is reacting to me so terribly because I've been a lousy daughter-in-law—I knew this would come back at me some day.* However, John later reminded me that for Alzheimer's victims, agitation is often escalated when they pick up on the emotional state of another individual.

Finally, I was able to fathom that Impie's vulnerability and need for support was bringing gifts to me—the first of which was realizing she was no longer the person I had perceived but someone who had lived a long, mostly hard life to which she could sense an ending. Gaining perspective, I realized my insecurity was actually a reflection of hers, though we expressed it differently. While I thrashed around with my heart on my sleeve, oozing low self-esteem, Impie masked her lack of self-confidence with bravado and bluff. Locked into our perceptual fields, we avoided intimacy and the truth that we had loved each other awkwardly for many years. Eventually I learned that what we criticize in others is most often just a part of ourselves waiting to be revealed. In the nick of time before Impie died, compassion arrived to free me from my limited perceptions, allowing me to be more expansive in my caring and to include not only our extended family but humanity. In the last months of her life, Impie and I often held hands—she in her hospital bed and me in my favorite chair nearby. There, I would pray aloud for her forgiveness, and occasionally a tremor would pass through her failing body, making me think she was responding.

Now a grandmother, I watch myself relax the boundaries of my grandchildren's worlds just as Impie did, while the parents of our grandchildren roll their eyes heavenward, just as we did. In spite of the distance that existed between us, I trusted Impie's love and care for our children implicitly. She had earned the right to throw out structure for latitude, and so have I. The generations may adore grandchildren differently, but we are all necessary for offering new beings many flavors of love.

If your previous relationship with a parent or in-law has been lacking . . .

The aging of a relative can heighten your awareness of the really important aspects of family relationships. Like an old book read in the light of a new context, the person's words may suddenly hold different meanings or greater immediacy. Simultaneously, you might uncover unknown parts of yourself urging you to open your heart of compassion and fall in love again.

To reevaluate your view of family relationships in preparation for confronting an aging relative, consider the following questions:

- Do you have faith that relationships can change?
- Are you willing to see your role in any complex relationship with an older relative?
- Are you capable of forgiving others and yourself? Can you see the pain you cause others?
- Would you rather be right or happy?

———— COMING OF AGE PASSAGE ————
Recognizing without justifying or judging

The Funky Holiday Gift Exchange

One of the releases from the intensity of caregiving is dark humor, but what is hilarious to you may not be at all funny to others.

Believing it imperative to laugh during any arduous time in life, we felt our eldercare years should be no exception. There were many precedents for dark humor in our families. For example, during my elementary years, my dad had shown up pretending to be drunk at a PTA meeting in a packed school gymnasium at which Mom was presiding. Eyes popped and tongues wagged as a gaggle of parents forwarded sympathetic glances toward Mom. Slurring, Dad attempted to tell a joke while my mother feigned embarrassment by covering her face with her hands until the conclusion of his performance, when they both revealed that it had all been a prank.

Thus it was no surprise that when John and I were gasping for oxygen amidst eldercare tasks, our humor took on a little darkness. For instance, during the winter holidays, one of our customs with next-door neighbors was to give obnoxious gifts back and forth, each exchange worse, until someone either wore out or gave up. During one of these days, Dad came for brunch with our kids and their respective partners. Upon receiving from a neighbor a mounted deer head with crocheted eyes, we were about to hoist a white flag of surrender when our imaginations caught fire. We had an impulse to set Dad in a folding chair, encase him in a large plastic bag up to his chin, secure the bag with a red bow and tape a holiday star to his bald head, then deliver him to the neighbor's doorstep and run. Dad enthusiastically agreed to the caper, offering to ask, "What time is dinner?" when the door was opened. That year we won the competition.

It was in this spirit that John and I anticipated our upcoming family white elephant gift exchange, where we were to swap items no longer needed. With some second thoughts about our plot, we nevertheless decided to put in the gift exchange the ashes of Aunt Lyna, who had died two years before. After her request to do nothing with her ashes, we actually had forgotten they were still housed at the funeral home, until we got a call announcing we would be charged "rent" if we didn't pick up her remains within thirty days.

As grotesque as it seemed, we considered the prank an appropriate expression of Aunt Lyna's character. Married five times and never having had children, she was a free spirit most renowned for her wacky sense of humor, a virtue that helped her get through a stroke in her forties, a subsequent mastectomy, then the loss of an eye in an automobile accident. In our hearts, we believed she would laugh as hard as we would at such a practical joke.

On the evening of the event, the shoe box containing Aunt Lyna's ashes glowed in gold foil among the other offerings, guaranteed to be one of the first chosen. When our daughter-in-law Patti reached for it, I was suddenly struck with remorse, aware I had expected one of our own children would claim it. A trooper, Patti remained stoic, uttering not a word while unwrapping the package. Her husband was more verbal, calling the gift "distasteful." Only our son-in-law Bill provided redemption for us as he grasped his sides in raucous laughter.

Based on percentages, John and I should have known our white elephant maneuver was high risk by the time we related it to a few close friends. Though all laughed heartily, their expressions of amusement were intermingled with shock. While I could justify an off-the-wall approach because of my family legacy, we should probably have given more consideration to the fact that the event involved many families with different backgrounds.

If your attempts to rescue yourself with humor fail to amuse others . . .

Humor often has the capacity to heal, especially amidst the gravity of eldercare. If you are a primary caretaker, and even if you're not, the shape of your humor might exceed the margins of general acceptability. Many professionals who deal with the dying are well aware of this propensity and anticipate close family members getting "a little crazy" while weighed down with sadness. If you feel uncomfortable expressing your inner comic to others, perhaps keep a journal or create therapeutic artwork containing humor.

As you discover ways to bring humor into your eldercare experiences, consider the following questions:

- Should you develop criteria for humor during eldercare duty?

- Can you allow others to have their own reaction to what you deem humorous? How will you avoid getting pulled into defensiveness or shame if they don't see things the way you do?

- Can you use the conflict that might arise from different tastes in humor among family members to learn more about the cast of characters in your family? Is it possible to apply this information in future interactions?

—— COMING OF AGE PASSAGE ——
Trusting time will heal

"If All of You Were Drowning, I'd Rescue the Dog!"

Don't underestimate the family pet. The value of pets in an elder's life increases as the family nest empties.

Though golf was the only sport Dad ardently pursued, my brothers and I were delighted when he would fulfill his promise to go swimming with us at the lake where we vacationed each summer. When he was fully immersed at last, wearing his plaid trunks, one of us would chide, "Daddy, if we were all drowning which of us would you rescue?" His answer was always the same. "I would just swim in circles. You would all drown because I could never make a choice!" Each of us knew that Dad wished to love the three of us as equitably as possible although we all believed there were times he did have favorites.

Much later, gathered for Mom's sixty-seventh birthday, our extended families had layered the walnut sideboard with packages of all sizes, one of which was a shoe box bound with a fuchsia satin ribbon to be opened last by her grandchildren's request. As Mom untied the box, the tiny head of a silver, sleepy puppy emerged, causing Mom to cry with joy. She had longed for another dog ever since their Great Dane had died years earlier, but my father had protested, "No more dog hair, no more cleaning up poop, no more barking in the night." But now the family had decided to risk overriding him. Although Dad kept his verbal reactions to himself, the corrugated veins popping out of his neck expressed his displeasure, which luckily disappeared in the weeks that followed. Consequently, my parents shared seven happy years with this spunky canine dubbed Sassy, before Mom died.

Soon after my mother's death, Dad began choreographing his day according to Sassy's feeding schedule and often only participated in family events if Sassy could be accommodated. Sassy nest-ed in the passenger seat when Dad ran errands or took a Sunday drive, traveled with him to visit old friends in Portland and Seattle, gobbled premium canned dog food, and enjoyed unlimited access to furniture or treats from the dinner table.

One tepid afternoon I observed on Dad's lap an overheated dog atop a soggy towel encapsulating the remains of a tray of ice cubes. "She's a hot dog," Dad wisecracked. But as Sassy's panting became more labored, he was clearly worried. Wanting to lighten up his mood, I joked, "Dad, what would you do if all of your kids were drowning and Sassy too?"

He barely hesitated before answering. "To be honest . . . I'd rescue the dog!" That evening, I shared the story by phone with my brothers.

Though we knew there was risk involved in bringing an animal into our elderly parents' lives, the dog ultimately filled many needs for both my mother and father. As her adult children and grandchildren grew more independent, Sassy made it possible for my aging mother to fulfill her need to care for others. And ironically, even though it was Dad who had rejected the idea of another dog, he thrived on the companionship Sassy provided following Mom's death.

Cognizant of the difference Sassy made in my parents' lives, John and I began taking our own dog Ellie to John's mother's house. Petting Ellie, we found, helped Impie break through her Alzheimer's fog and predictably calmed her agitation.

If you have a parent who is failing, lonely, or without access to nurturance . . .

Today, pet therapy is a popular service for elders. Professionals have determined that pets provide older people with many physical, emotional, mental, and spiritual benefits, including companionship, brain stimulation, an established routine, the chance to exercise, and a purpose for being more involved with life. Further, research has shown that a pet can prolong the time an elder stays in their home before relocating to a care facility.

The appropriateness of an elder having a pet depends on several variables, such as the receptivity of others involved and the mental and physical condition of the person. If you decide to bring a dog into your parent's home, choose a mature neutered dog that is housebroken and unlikely to roam. A good place to begin looking for an older animal is at local pet shelters or canine-assisted living programs. For help with the selection process, consider seeking the counsel of a dog training professional with experience in pet-assisted therapy.

To prepare for the possibility of providing your parent with a pet, consider the following questions:

- Do you think your parent would be receptive to and capable of having a relationship with a pet?

- Would it be advisable to hire a professional to assess the situation and determine the appropriateness of a pet in your parent's life?

- If your parent has a caregiver, are they receptive to adding an animal to their daily routines? Does your parent or the caregiver have preferences or disdain for certain types of animals?

- If you anticipate moving your parent into a retirement community or assisted living, have you researched the facility's policies regarding pets or pet therapy?

———— COMING OF AGE PASSAGE ————

Broadening perspectives on resources for love

The Family Plot That Flopped

If your parent procrastinates in end-of-life planning, it could leave your family with a residue of confusion and regret.

All his life John's father Ray said his heart ached at the mention of his mother, who died of lead poisoning when he was five years old. Spurned by a disapproving stepmother who lavished her attention on a new child, Ray left home at age sixteen bent on resurrecting the "sweet maternal." In stark contrast to the alienation emerging from this branch of his family tree, John's mother Impie's family was tribal. His four doting aunts lavished him with love. In fact, the five sisters stayed so closely connected that they purchased a family plot at the local cemetery.

Another family plot thickened when his parents individually told John their end-of-life wishes. Ray aspired to be buried next to his birth mother, two hundred miles away, while Impie wanted to share space with her sisters in the hometown cemetery. Confused, John put these confidences in a drawer labeled "I'll figure this out later."

Over time, when Ray's health began to fail, he reiterated his burial plans to Impie, urging, "You can join me there eventually, darling."

"I think Mom was hoping you'd both be buried in the same cemetery as her sisters, Dad," John intervened.

Shaking his head, Ray made a second appeal to Impie, explaining, "I've already purchased the spaces. You'll do this for me, won't you, sweetheart?" Impie gave him the nod of deferment she had perfected during five decades of wifely subservience.

Soon after, Ray died and was laid to rest beside his mother in a corner of northern Washington. Afterwards, as the autumn sky threatened rainfall, John brooded while we wound our way through a rural landscape. When we fell into bed that night, I knew he had shifted his focus to Impie as he muttered to himself, "Doesn't matter what anybody else thinks. Dad was shortsighted, and Mom can hardly figure out how to get food to her mouth. We just need to arrive at the 'best right.'"

More than nine years later, John and his brothers lowered their mother's ashes into the parcel adjoining their dad's, opting to honor Ray's overt wish rather than attempt to translate Impie's ambiguity. Having come to an agonizing consensus, they envisioned her spirit as loyal and Ray's as finally secure, alongside his two mothers—the one who bore him and the one who later married and took care of him.

In retrospect, the brothers recalled missed opportunities for resolving the delicate matter of final planning. Always, it seemed, they had opted to put the subject off until another day.

When vagueness clouds your parent's final wishes . . .

Prevent conflict and confusion among family members by encouraging your parent to document and communicate their end-of-life wishes well in advance of their final days. If your parent refuses or procrastinates until too late, you and other family members can make the best decisions possible based on your parent's value system and personality.

To help your parent be specific about end-of-life wishes or prepare yourself to make the decisions for them, consider the following questions:

- Has your parent stated their burial wishes to a family member? If not, does your parent want you and your siblings to make these decisions for them posthumously?

- Do you and your siblings have consensus on this matter? If not, how could you reach an agreement?

- Are any decisions colored by childhood competitions or resentments?

- Are you prepared to make peace with an ambiguous outcome?

———— COMING OF AGE PASSAGE ————

Living with ambiguity

Ashes to Ashes and Dust to . . . Dumpster

When your parent makes an end-of-life wish with potentially lasting impact on the family, you may regret holding your tongue.

Hours after my mother died, my dad, brother, and I visited the funeral home where she was to be cremated. She had long before established there was to be no grave, no crypt, and no memorial or service, so we anticipated having to take care of very few routine details. But after the funeral director gathered information for the obituary, obtained signatures, and arranged for the death certificate, we were startled by his final question: "And how would you like her ashes?"

"Hell, I don't want 'em! They're all mixed up with everybody else's anyway," Dad blurted out.

Locking anguished eyes over Dad's head, my brother and I said, "Well, this really is his decision."

The director slipped our file under his arm then marched toward the stairs, saying, "So, they'll be in a cardboard box. We'll let you know when they're ready to be picked up." But my brother and I knew Dad had no intention of ever retrieving this box.

Returning home, we were greeted by relatives. My mother's sister asked, "When will you pick up Jeannie's remains?" Casting my eyes to the linoleum, I hoped my brother would volunteer that Mom was probably on her way to the dump, but he didn't so I did. Auntie turned white, and during the rest of the afternoon she and other relatives unobtrusively scanned the premises for small reminders of Mom they could keep as mementos.

Weeks later, a collection was taken at the elementary school where Mom had volunteered for forty-three years, and a bronze plaque commemorating her contributions was subsequently displayed in the lobby. Thus, by default our family acquired a public memorial to Mom.

Dad's sentiments surprised me. Always one to take death in stride, insisting in the case of Mom's that "it had to happen someday," he poured his sorrow into the commemoration proceedings, selecting the verse to be carved beside his beloved's name and pestering the engraver until the etching was just right. Then almost daily for the rest of his life, he walked the quarter mile to the elementary school to commune with Mom.

I, too, welcomed this tribute. Though I had been reared to not let death upset me, each time someone close to me died I unconsciously committed myself to a life sentence of unexpressed grief. And the bronze plaque honoring Mom became a place for softening, for letting go of pent-up anguish and feeling close to her. Even so, I occasionally placed a red rose atop the green dumpster near the funeral home, where I swore I heard Mom's laughter.

If your parent wishes to be cremated . . .

The amount of grief some families attempt to avoid could fill Crater Lake. Though the reasons parents give for going on after their death—"Spare the family," "Don't fuss over me"—sound altruistic, repressed grief combined with the loss of a parent can wreak havoc on the psyche. Therefore, part of coming of age requires the expression of remorse.

If your parent has a desire to be cremated, don't leave the final arrangements to the funeral parlor. Instead, personalize the decision by having your parent put their wishes in writing then doing some soul-searching of your own. To prepare for this contingency, consider the following questions:

- What does your parent want done with the ashes—have them placed in an urn and buried, deposited in a colum barium, scattered? Where and by whom?
- If your parent has no preferences, whom would they like to make these decisions?
- If your parent requests no memorial service or site for the ashes, how will you achieve closure after their death?

——— COMING OF AGE PASSAGE ———
Transcending stoicism to express sorrow

The Motley Memorial

If you and your siblings have diverse philosophies, arriving at common ground regarding your parent's memorial may be a formidable task requiring a reassessment of expectations.

When Impie's death drew John and his brothers to the family home, their differences, largely dormant during the decade spent supporting their mother, emerged again as they planned her memorial. The first arrangements were made virtually without problems. Since the three siblings shared no common religious or spiritual underpinnings, they secured a church the family attended in the early years. Then it was decided each, together with one of the grandchildren, would speak at the service, and the Ladies' Auxiliary consented to host a reception following the memorial, in exchange for only a small honorarium.

However, the semblance of unity evaporated when the pastor asked, "And what about scripture? Music?" Charles, the most intellectual of the trio, was open to any format but wished to fill the chapel with somber classical music before, during, and after the memorial. John leaned toward a more spiritual approach, with generic readings giving way to the uplifting strains of a harp. Joe, a fundamentalist, preferred scripture from the New Testament.

In the end, the audience first heard the wisdom of Deepak Chopra, the Gospel mostly according to John, and piano improvisations of Mozart's Requiem and Bach's Cantata 118, followed by two taped selections by a Christian vocalist and a CD rendition of *House at Pooh Corner* intended to remind everyone of Impie's devotion to her four grandchildren. Finally, four summaries of her life were given, no two of which portrayed the same woman. While leaving the chapel, John noticed bewilderment in the eyes of those who remained. Regarding it as a mirror of the sentiment he shared with his siblings, he wondered if they would stay connected.

While two brothers had the desire to start anew, unfortunately the third isolated himself, making it impossible for them to achieve resolution before returning to their respective homes. Those who transcended their differences sensed the opportunity to deepen their bond, recognizing they were capable of finding inner peace.

If you and your siblings are juggling contrasting perspectives while planning a memorial service for a parent . . .

If philosophical and religious differences in your family cannot be resolved, it is nevertheless possible to avoid the pull of conditioned responses and begin reconstructing relationships. The first step is to develop more tolerance, both together in family meetings and privately in support groups. This work offers many possibilities for personal growth and family healing that may last beyond the eldercare years. If some family members refuse to participate, be prepared to accept that this is their choice.

To prepare your family to work together when a parent dies, consider the following questions:

- Can you and your siblings address your differences in advance so they won't result in conflicts when your parent dies and the emotional stakes are high?

- Can you and your siblings work cohesively toward respecting one another's needs while attempting to meet your own?

- If a dilemma cannot be resolved, could you commit to releasing your expectations and transcend the circumstances?

—— COMING OF AGE PASSAGE ——
Being tolerant of others' values

Stuff and Money

Being kept in the dark about your parent's estate plans can lead to an unexpected inheritance of misunderstanding or hurt feelings.

In my family, since everyone understood that our parents' estate would be meager, my siblings and I joked among ourselves about our inheritances getting us through tough times in the future. Then tales from friends destined to receive ample bequests convinced us our situation could be a blessing in disguise. Besides, our parents' collection to be divided up contained a number of amazing antiques, including a delightful oil-painting advertisement that had once belonged to our grocer grandfather, portraying a St. Bernard accompanying a diminutive young woman carrying a lunch box and captioned "To School Well-Fed on Grape-Nuts."

Dad had made it clear that after he and Mom had died, he would prefer we get an appraiser to give estimates on items of value then take turns choosing things, seeing to it that the dollar amount remains equitable. Mom, on the other hand, began writing names on the backs of pictures and the bottoms of antiques a few years before her death, something we discovered when Kaaren picked up a milk glass kitten displaying her name. Previously we all knew Kip would get the grandfather clock, Ed would receive the jukebox, and I would inherit two generations worth of silverware, but we had no idea Mom had surreptitiously established her own dispersal system.

During the family holidays that followed, my brothers and I mimed looking for our names on various items, kidding each other, although there were a few unmarked possessions with significant sentiment for each of us, such as the advertisement of the Grape-Nuts girl. A nineteenth-century sideboard fashioned from burled walnut panels, the most valuable item, never bore anyone's name. Since it appeared too large for any of our homes, we thought about giving it to Kaaren and Bill, the next generation of antique collectors in the family.

Inevitably, the time came for us all to select possessions. Kip and I made hypothetical plans to share Grandpa's oil painting until we turned it over and found Kaaren's name in Mom's handwriting.

Then my sister-in-law Bev discovered that the sideboard would just fit in our dining room after all. I was overwhelmed when the rest of the family said, "Yes, take it. Just never give it away or sell it."

In the end, generosity reigned, although if our parents had had more assets or priceless possessions conflict may have dominated. Today, each of us is delighted to come upon a remembrance of Mom and Dad when we visit one another. Grandma Gladder's oil painting of pansies is highlighted at Kip and Bev's; the jukebox, in Ed and Kelly's new restaurant; the family rocking chairs, at Greg and Patti's; the oil painting of the Grape-Nuts girl, at Bill and Kaaren's; and the sideboard and baby photos of Mom and Dad, at our home.

If you fear that the allocation of family money or possessions will wreak havoc in your family . . .

Receiving an inheritance or treasured possessions symbolizing parents and early life, can be a healing experience that facilitates grief. Because this is so, when parents allocate possessions wisely as part of end-of-life planning, they spare their family great sorrow and provide them a legacy family members can cherish throughout life.

One of the most difficult challenges for an adult child is to experience inequity in the distribution of a parent's bequeathments. Unequal allocation, even if it entails compensation for something such as investment in one person's college education, can feel like rejection; even worse is to be surprised. In the best circumstances, the parent will have explained any imbalances to those concerned. If you suspect your parent has not considered potential complications, raise these issues (see Appendix A, especially pages 224–225, for more information).

There are many ways a parent can divest money or property to heirs. They can, among other things, decide and document who gets what; let heirs determine how to divvy up funds and possessions, including the possibility of selling all assets and sharing the proceeds; and choose an impartial executor of the will or suggest an independent appraiser to facilitate distribution.

To prepare for the implications of inheritance, consider the following questions:

- Do you and your siblings share similar expectations regarding the distribution of your parent's belongings?

- Rather than possessions and money, is there something else you need from your parent that you can still get, such as reassurance of their love and high regard for you?

- If tensions arise regarding particular bequeathings, what creative solutions might help you and your siblings reframe the experience of "getting"? If a sibling seems attached to an item you've received, would you consider giving it to them?

———— COMING OF AGE PASSAGE ————

Discovering mutual wealth in inheritance

Surviving the Annual Family Reunion

As your parents' generation passes, you have an opportunity to renew and appreciate family bonds.

In late summer, my deceased mother's family and I followed our ancestral bread crumbs to Montana for a family reunion. Preparing to spend two days with family farmers and fundamentalists, ex-hippies and ministers, right-wing extremists and bleeding hearts, teachers, doctors, salespeople, career ice skaters, technicians, psychologists, opportunists, malcontents, and skeletons, I held my breath.

My stomach tightened as John and I arrived at the lake and began infiltrating this caucus of kin. Studying the participants, I questioned what I had in common with them, how we could possibly be related.

In the hours that followed, I erupted spontaneously with grandparent stories and listened with glee as others recited legends of their own. We all chortled as a family member forgot he was no longer a kid and dove into the shallow end of the lake, surfacing unscathed; and we giggled when a cousin with swimmer's ear plugged his ear with Silly Putty so he could justify water-skiing, failing to realize his body heat would soften the mass. I rode in the sidecar of a Harley-Davidson, volunteered to judge a watermelon-eating contest for the family's youngest generation, got ravaged by swarms of mosquitoes, ate too much, and scarcely slept. I laughed and I cried . . . for what was no longer and what I suspected I had missed.

Leaving the reunion, we traced the riverbeds of my ancestors through the Rocky Mountains and returned home. I remarked to John, "I've tried so hard not be one of them, you know? But I am . . . aren't I? And I'm not."

If you have become disconnected from your family of origin . . .

After my family's reunion, I concluded that surviving the affair was not the problem. The challenge was instead in letting go, rediscovering the uniqueness of each person, and enjoying the stories as part of the family heritage—making the legends live again. Looking back, I noted my resistance in claiming a space among the branches of my family tree; looking forward, I saw myself as one of many small but vital links in a lineage contributing to the evolution of humanity.

If you have lost connection with your kin over the years because of geographical separation, lifestyle differences, or personality clashes, you may be missing out on potentially rewarding relationships. Though you may feel you no longer have much in common with these relatives, your mutual history binds you with them in ways not possible with new relationships. In addition, shared family history not only cements connections between relatives, it creates a cultural context that helps furnish a sense of identity and destiny.

To better assess your connection with blood relatives, consider the following questions:

- If you have minimized or eliminated contact with your family, was your decision necessary as part of your development to maturity?

- If you have little in common with certain relatives, have you tried alternative ways to be together? For instance, if conversation seems difficult, can you find an activity to share?

- Are some relationships truly not worth the effort? Are you willing to accept this circumstance rather than feel guilty about loss of connection with these relatives?

———— COMING OF AGE PASSAGE ————
Coveting family

Catch and Release

When there is no relief from family strife, you may need to surrender.

Many studies today indicate that siblings are overwhelmingly the most important source of interpersonal stress for caregivers. As such, eldercare can challenge your family myths about connection with siblings and other family members and force you to find ways to transform perspectives and relationships.

Coming down the homestretch of our years in eldercare, John and I were able to trace the ways in which each caregiver among our relatives either fell back into unhealthy childhood patterns or grew from the experience. As for us, overall we had been successful, made surprising discoveries about ourselves, and forged new bonds with our parents and other family members, having honored our parents' wishes to the best of our abilities. However, wounds from early childhood continuing into adulthood took their toll in some relationships, with one family member unconsciously or intentionally hurting another and consequently having to work on negative behavior patterns. Frequently we discovered love lying dormant beneath anger, blame, or misunderstanding, allowing those involved to eventually come to a better understanding of their dynamics.

Of everyone involved in our two families, John tried the hardest to express generosity of spirit, but from one relative in particular he endured criticism that bordered on abuse. We consulted with eldercare specialists when it became clear that in assuming a role formerly played by another relative John had changed his family's dynamics and ignited an inferno. During one session, John broadened his perspective on the situation when an adviser remarked, "Your relative's behavior regarding your mother's in-home caregivers wouldn't be tolerated in a nursing home. Can you see how you are trying to be this person's counselor?"

Coincidentally, at the time the emotional intensity in John's family was peaking, the two of us were involved in a training program that supported the expression of previously repressed feelings. Hence, whenever John felt crazy in dealing with the difficult relationship with his relative he was able to practice transforming his anger and achieve emotional release. In this cathartic process he became a model for me, an ironic occurrence in a world where women have more permission than men to express feelings.

Through working with his anger, John was able to transcend patterns he and his incensed relative had enacted for decades. When his kin attacked with white-hot anger, rather than sticking around for punishment John was able to say, "I'm not going to talk to you until you've done some work on your rage." And when this relative appeared unable to work toward an acceptable, adult relationship, John ceased operating under the illusion that things could be fixed. He learned how to discern between parts of an issue that were his and parts having nothing to do with him. Thus he was able to rise above conflict rather than staying mired in agitation and resentment.

Another gift of John's newfound insight was the realization that he could not rescue or be rescued, that every life's journey holds suffering from which there is no protection but also that all humans have inner endowments allowing them to reach out to a higher source. After trying to control family circumstances and force relationships to a new level of maturity, he saw the necessity for releasing himself and others from the ties that bound them and trusting that healing would happen in its own time. He learned that some relationships cannot be rehabilitated and are better surrendered to therapy, prayer, and faith. Laying down his caregiving mantle, he commenced the long journey of detaching with compassion—of setting aside his expectations without casting judgment, of allowing. Now, he had opened the way to fully grieve the loss of his mother without feeling he had to take care of the rest of the family.

If you are dealing with difficult family relationships . . .

Because siblings and other family members can resort to child-hood behaviors during eldercare, there are numerous opportunities at such times to enter into conflict, including disagreements about guardianship of your parent, moving your parent into a nursing home, or participating in their end-of-life planning. Yearning for an ideal relationship with your kin is understandable but may be unre-alistic. Although crises involving an aging parent can draw siblings closer together in the moment, it is wise not to have false expecta-tions about the perpetuation of such bonds and goodwill.

If you are stuck in unresolved conflict with a family member, consider the following questions:

- Are you in a no-win situation?

- Can you see the role, attitudes, and behavior you are enact-ing that support the status quo?

- Are you willing to act on your self-knowledge and take a position that might help you transcend old patterns?

- If unsuccessful in mending a relationship, can you let it go in the spirit of love, leaving the door open for renewal?

——— COMING OF AGE PASSAGE ———
Letting it be

PART 5 ——
Higher Altitudes

As in most odysseys, John and I failed to perceive the gifts of eldercare until we were broken and humbled enough to realize that not only were our parents passing but we ourselves were being given precious opportunities for transformation and growth. Rising to each new occasion and welcoming infusions of faith, we were forced to grow, leaving our egos behind, or at least depriving them of a little oxygen. Finally, the spiritual realm opened wide its arms, permanently altering our awareness as we ascended to unforeseen heights of understanding.

After the passing of more elders, John and I experienced a new interconnectedness with our current relatives, our ancestors, and future generations, recognizing all were a part of a much larger family. It was as though eldercare had carried us into thick undergrowth, and not until we thrashed our way back to the clearing could we embrace the streams of light awaiting us.

Living intimately with family members as they complete their lives teaches some of the privileged secrets of mortality—how to heal old hurts, how to be present and give voice to self-expression, and how to brim over with thankfulness for the chance to deepen our understanding, make a difference, and sur-

render to death. In healing old injuries, you become more forgiving and compassionate. By being present and articulate in
each moment of eldercare, you discover how to not only survive
difficult circumstances but see them as growth promoting. Filling
with gratitude, you suddenly feel yourself wrapped snugly in the
warm blanket of grace.

Mirror of Mourning

When a parent is dying, you have an opportunity to face yourself.

In the weeks following my mother's stroke, I spent mornings at the rehabilitation center pinching Mom's paralyzed toes and praying for signs of improvement. By the second month, there were only slight changes in her condition—she was awake more but speaking was difficult. There was little to do but just be with her, celebrating who she was and contemplating who I was as her daughter.

Being in her presence and reflecting on her life, I felt voyeuristic when aides changed her gown or bathed her, since throughout the years she had concealed her body from me. As I now peeked at her splayed on a mattress, her breasts looked like those of a young woman, in contrast to her corrugated throat. I recalled moments the year before when she had described bending over to dry her legs after bathing only to observe her bosoms hanging like cucumbers, and how she had confessed to sprouting hair in places it had never been while losing masses in regions of former high growth. Set off from her snow-white head, a few dark wisps of hair could now be seen growing from her chin.

I evoked an image of how Mom looked as she first emerged from anesthesia, attempting to cover the hole in her face typically filled with dentures. As the years passed, I reminded myself, Mom endured rather than accepted the assault age makes on our dignity.

Now, in the rehab facility, I couldn't get enough of her, realizing her breath might be extinguished at any moment. My eyes traced the nostrils I had gazed at vertically as a child, the low forehead, crooked chin, sloping shoulders, thick arms, small feet, the saddlebag hips we shared. I thought back on family photographs stored in boxes: Mom in a two-piece bathing suit at Bangs Lake near Chicago, slender from days of chasing two small children; her radiance in her "go to hell" black dress en route to a party with Dad; the hugeness of her belly just before she gave birth to my ten-pound, six-ounce baby brother. In later years Mom had ceased her long-waged war to fit society's gender definitions for attractiveness, while Dad, especially after seeing a pretty woman golfer on the links, would mumble, "It's too bad your mother let herself go," explaining that though men retained their good looks after fifty, few women did. Annoyed, I realized how quietly Mom had borne her suffering.

There I was, at age fifty-one myself, holding my mother's mottled hand, stroking the stubble on her legs, massaging her thinning scalp, and tracing the flat warts on her back. With only two decades separating us, she exposed a part of my future, forecasting my experiences to come.

As dusk crept into Mom's west window the night before she died, I wept with gratitude for the way her aging body documented her tenacious spirit and a life well lived. In this moment, I was simultaneously aware of our similar and dissimilar life experiences.

If you are spending time with a parent who may have only a short time to live . . .

The death of a parent is a formidable loss, causing the most composed of us as well as those carrying anger from the past to experience great sadness. Since most of us do not grieve for the little losses in life, even those perceived as positive—such as disconnections from loved ones when patterns of contact have been disrupted, from peers following job promotions, and from our former sense of identity after branching off in a new direction—we often are unprepared for the big losses. Understandably, the impending death of a parent can challenge all our resources.

Although many parents share the wish to die quickly, preferably during sleep, most are likely to linger. Still, a prolonged death can have advantages for caregivers, offering them time to come to terms with the transition, further cultivate their relationship with their parents, as well as face their own life choices and eventual mortality.

If you are present for a parent's last days, as you bear witness consider the following questions:

- Are you aware of feelings surfacing as you acknowledge your parent is preparing to leave? Are you expressing them?
- What have you learned about yourself, your parent, and death as a result of caregiving?
- Is there any unfinished business from your past that, for your own peace of mind, needs to be faced before your parent's death? ·

———— COMING OF AGE PASSAGE ————
Embracing bondage

Cited with Suicide

When the gap between longevity and quality of life widens, a parent may become so desperate that suicide seems a viable alternative.

Having prostate surgery at age eighty-five was an emotional as well as physical ordeal for my father, and the month after surgery was especially tough. Unable to comprehend the tangle of tubing strapped to his calf, he seemed convinced one catheter transported both his urine and his bowel movements when in fact the single tube was inserted in his urinary tract to allow passage of fluids. No amount of explaining could steer him away from his conclusion. The real difficulty, however, was less about the technicalities than about adjusting to them. Rarely did Dad appear in public now, and when he did he'd grasp at his private parts fearing the catheter would fall off or people might notice the unwieldy bulge in his sweatpants. Worse, no amount of vigilance could spare him repeated pain from the tugs and pokes of his catheter each time he moved.

Fortunately, we did enjoy some light moments together, like the first time I attempted to change his catheter and it popped apart, spraying us both. When horror gave way to laughter, my father remarked, "We never told you this, honey, but your mother and I were a little frightened when you were thinking about becoming a nurse."

Also during the month after surgery Dad lost nearly thirty pounds and had to punch new holes in his belt to keep his trousers up. I asked if he was trying to starve himself to death. "No," he replied, "it's just hard to eat." Subsequent X rays revealed a small blockage in his esophagus inhibiting his ability to swallow. When the X-ray attendant recommended he see a rehabilitation therapist to improve his ability to swallow, Dad folded his arms over his chest and asked to be taken home instead.

Before falling asleep that night, I lamented, *How could I have accused him of trying to take his life? The poor man is obviously losing weight because his whole system is falling apart.* The next morning I began pureeing his food and encouraging him to eat.

Another day when I arrived Dad was holding his breath and staring at his watch. Unsettled, I took his face in my hands, asking, "Dad, is there something you are hoping to accomplish by holding your breath?"

He didn't miss a beat, declaring, "I will get to have a heart attack because my body is so weak now."

I sighed. "And what if that doesn't work, Dad?"

He replied, "There are bullets in my gun. Or I could drink Drano or jam golf balls down my windpipe. But I'd prefer a heart attack."

I suggested antidepressants, suspecting he had long been overwhelmed by his loss of independence. He gave me one of his are-you-out-of-your-mind gazes and turned away. Despair had set in, and he refused to consult a medical professional.

Soon after, an informed friend paid Dad a visit. Sharing his wish to die, Dad explained, "I don't want to be a burden anymore. I can't see, can barely chew, my hearing's gone, and I can't pee. Enough. Each morning I wake in a cold sweat, terrified that I must face another day. What did I do to deserve this?" His friend asserted that by starving himself Dad would only draw out his dying because he was still well hydrated.

Dad relinquished his mission and returned to three square meals a day. Wedged between the will to live and the wish to die, he endured another three years.

My father fit the profile of the type of elder inclined to take things into his own hands if ever he became incapacitated or mired in suffering. Our family had long understood that with diminished dignity or the sense of being a burden to loved ones, he would find a way to end his life.

When it became apparent Dad was committed to dying on his own terms, we resolved to respect his actions and be there for him emotionally, regardless of the outcome. We shared our decision with him, adding that we would, however, not be willing to assist him in any plans to end his life, and mindful that we would have to deal with the aftermath, we begged him not to use his gun. We also cautioned him against an unsuccessful suicide attempt likely to diminish his quality of life.

At first, we were nervous about offering support for fear he might think we were wishing him to die, but instead he shared tears of gratitude. Although momentarily reassured, we knew there were no guarantees that he would hold up his end of the agreement.

To our knowledge, during the three years he lingered he never attempted suicide, although he continued to reserve the option. Despite the solidarity following our response to the ending my father contemplated, many questions remain. Was it God's will or his friend's intervention that prompted him to withdraw his intentions of suicide? Did he ultimately celebrate or regret his decision? There are no easy answers to such inquiries, only truths revealed through soul-searching, reflection, and faith.

If you suspect your parent is contemplating suicide . . .

The thought of a parent harboring death wishes can leave you feeling painfully helpless. However, facing the possibility will prepare you to take a more active part in the situation should it arise. Evaluate whether your parent might succumb to real or imagined death wishes, then plan your best approach. If it turns out that your fears are imagined, chalk up the experience as an exercise in discernment. If they prove to be real, it's time for a heart-to-heart talk to let your parent know your views and encourage your parent to reveal their inner thoughts.

As our society debates the morality of euthanasia and assisted suicide, technology is affording so many people the option to extend life that Americans are living longer today than ever before—developments complicating the questions families are raising with ethicists, healthcare providers, counselors, and theologians. Meanwhile, prompted by legal restrictions and a healthcare system bound by the tradition of sustaining life at all costs, a significant number of elders are quietly laying groundwork for ending their own lives if necessary. As members of a generation that prided itself on independence, they are well aware that even with laws in place some doctors will unofficially supply doses of narcotics while others will provide a referral to the Hemlock Society, a nonprofit association that supports choice and dignity at the end of life. A large percentage of elders will appeal to a friend or family member for assistance.

Confronting the possibility of an elder's suicide is a profound coming of age transition for adult children. Suddenly you perceive yourself no longer as a victim of life "happening" to you but as a player in a huge unfolding. For help in accessing the real or imagined possibility of elder suicide, consider the following questions:

- Is your parent refusing food and water? In healthcare circles, when someone has a terminal disease there is nothing unethical or suicidal about their refusal to take in nutrition and water, as indicated in a communications alert issued in July 2003 by the National Hospice and Palliative Care Organization: "A patient's right is supported to choose care or refuse unwanted medical intervention including the provision of artificially supplied hydration and nutrition. Since nutritional and hydration needs of patients actively dying are different from the needs of a person in good health, as death nears, the body begins to 'shut down' and food and fluid requirements decrease. Of the 885,000 patients served by the 3,200 hospice providers in the nation [a 2002 statistic] a very small number of clients chose this approach."

- Do you suspect your parent might be suffering from a mental disorder such as dementia or depression? If so, has the parent consulted a physician or psychiatrist?

- Are your parent's thoughts of suicide sporadic or deliberated? Are you hearing a cry for help? If so, has this cry just begun or has it become intensified over time? Is your parent's inclination based on rational thinking reinforced by valid, up-to-date information?

- Does your parent adhere to religious beliefs? If not, would your parent consider seeking spiritual support to transcend their current state of mind?

- Do you choose to accept or stifle a suicide intention? What are your beliefs about the ethics of suicide?

———— COMING OF AGE PASSAGE ————
Living without absolutes

Purging Purgatory

If you hope to influence your parent's spiritual outlook as death approaches, first decide who you are praying for.

As I witnessed my agnostic father bargaining with God while awaiting death, my stomach clenched. Never having established a solid religious or spiritual foundation, Dad was grasping at Catholic straws from memories of his childhood neighbors. He clung to the idea of purgatory, adamant there were occurrences in his life for which he would be required to do penance. And although over the years he had upheld certain principles, such as being faithful to Mom, never selling a policyholder more life insurance than necessary, and remaining true to his strong political convictions, he firmly believed that none of these elements would excuse him from punishment for his misdeeds.

More than anything, I wanted to relieve him of his incriminations. First, I tried persuading him to accept my version of God—a source or higher power I saw as loving rather than punitive. He didn't buy it; in his view, he was going to be chastised and would face it like a man.

Next, I sought to introduce spiritual perspectives by reading to him from such books as *Conversations with God* by Neale Donald Walsch, in which God invites us to awaken to answers within us and to create reality instead of inheriting it. But Dad would sleep through the recitations, often snoring loudly.

Finally, I prayed, fervently requesting that Dad learn to be gentler with himself and acknowledge his goodness. As my pleas took on the urgency of commando edicts, I became increasingly aware that I could not counter God's will, for either my father or myself.

Having been very judgmental of people who over the years attempted to impose their beliefs on me, I was now endeavoring to do the same to my father—overtly to "save" him and covertly to abort the pain his questioning caused me. I wanted Dad's ending to leave me peaceful rather than agitated. I also thought I knew better; I was sure that since my spiritual beliefs had given me a deep faith, they could work for him, too. Ultimately realizing that Dad had always been a self-learner who trusted his own answers more than anyone else's, I had to simply allow him his beliefs and surrender to the eventual consequences.

Of course, Dad's passing was nothing like I imagined. Speechless from a stroke, he departed in silence, carrying with him the mystery of his relationship to a higher being.

If you are personally invested in your parent's spiritual experience as they approach death . . .

During eldercare, it is a good idea to reflect on your spiritual values and how they may or may not harmonize with your parent's religious views. Also contemplate the possible implications of this for any end-of-life decisions, possible posthumous memorials for your parent, and especially your own closure regarding their eventual death. If possible, discuss these issues with your parent to gain peace of mind regarding their outlook. But whether or not discussions ensue, be tolerant of your parent's beliefs and avoid using eldercare as an excuse to influence your parent's spiritual choices.

To prepare for your parent's eventual death as respectfully as possible, ask yourself these questions and allow them to lead you to others:

- Are you doing your spiritual work through your parent or allowing them their own beliefs?
- Might you be projecting onto your parent your own fears or uncertainties about death?
- Do you have faith that your parent is in God's hands?

——— COMING OF AGE PASSAGE ———

Allowing

Mobilizing Faith

Sometimes you cannot circumvent loss but only gaze into it warmed by the remnants of faith.

While I was a young mother, my own mother and I shared intimacies and celebrated each other, but as I began to expand my social world I moved in new directions. More time elapsed between my visits with Mom, and we started avoiding topics like politics, child rearing, gender roles, and others that might lead to disagreement. My beliefs and behaviors became increasingly different from hers.

I felt both sadness and anger at the new distance between us and my mother's complaints about seldom seeing me anymore. Only years later did I realize my feelings were symptomatic of separation, a prerequisite for maturity.

Then two years before my mother's death in 1993, I wrote the following:

> My mom and I can watch movies together (*Thelma and Louise, Out of Africa*) that say things the gap between our generations disallows. This has been a delicate negotiation, for when I first began speaking my own truth she cowered and went away for too long. I choose not to be so noisy with her now; I am afraid she may die, and I want her presence for whatever time we have left. In a darkened room it is okay to let our secrets live in psychic Technicolor. When the lights come on, we return to our public spaces. Her mouth is always cross-stitched shut—but her blue eyes signal me.

> Now, my daughter Kaaren and I attend an occasional motion picture (*The Piano, Breaking the Waves*), offering sanctuary from our struggle to disengage. She has let the hair on her legs grow; I understand but am glad to see this disappear

into the blackness of the theater. I think and she feels as we absorb sounds and images. I notice her angry tears; she reaches for my hand. We don't speak much because of our language barrier. My throat is cross-stitched and hers is open.

In our town, there is a remarkable little restaurant converted from an old drugstore. I have spent hours there with my friends Barb and Sonya, pouring out, taking in. Sometimes I imagine my mom at a table across the room with her friends Lenora and Wilma, and my daughter atop a barstool with her university mates Lisa and Erica, while my maternal grandmother locks us into eye contact from a portrait mounted above the restored fountain. Together, we are part of a semiconscious evolution that presents the gift of our lives, our collective experience, to the next generations.

On January 7, 1993, Mom and I had anticipated a day-long drive from Spokane to Seattle, crossing Snoqualmie Pass to attend a family wedding. It had been many years since the two of us had shared extended time, and I was excited for the possibilities of connecting with her at a more mature level.

The evening before, however, the pass had closed due to avalanches. I called Mom over the dinner hour, and we started out marginally optimistic about navigating the mountainside the following day. Then I suggested we postpone the trip till spring, when we could congratulate the newlyweds in a less chaotic atmosphere. She agreed, but the disappointment in her voice was hard to bear.

On January 8, Mom had a stroke, and two months later she was gone.

Mom's death caught me midway in my development toward independence. Although we shared much affection during those two months, it was tinged with crisis. Not wanting her to think she was dying, I refrained from telling her of my sorrow over the breach we had endured. All I could articulate was how much I loved her.

For years following Mom's death, I lamented my failure to

rekindle the bond I'd remembered from childhood. The first year, I placed mementos of her around our home, trying to fill an empti- ness inside. I believed I had forfeited the opportunity for a closer relationship with Mom and now had to face the consequences. Daily I wrestled with demons.

Today, I continue to work on our relationship, feeling that Mom still exists spiritually. With renewed faith, I forgive myself and, address- ing my inadequacies, assert a willingness to see the ebbs and flows of our relationship as a reflection of being human, as part of a human chain of linked spirits trying their best in a disconnected world.

If your parent dies in the midst of your unfinished business . . .

Professionals in child development and psychology have long maintained that to mature, an individual must separate from their parents. Ideally, this journey commences at age two and is repeated more dramatically in adolescence, although sometimes it is post- poned, or the individual transfers attachment to other authority fig- ures who take the place of parents.

If you have a vulnerable or problematic relationship with a par- ent who may be facing death, consider the following questions:

- Do you understand the reasons for any problems in the relationship with your parent, in terms of personality differ- ences, the generation gap, or dissimilar values and beliefs?
- What unfinished business do you wish to conclude before your parent dies?
- Do you have spiritual beliefs that can help you sustain the difficulties in your parental relationship?
- Can you gain a wider perspective to see your family in the larger context of humanity?

——— COMING OF AGE PASSAGE ———

Calling upon faith to validate your experience

Holiday Visitation

Be alert to signs that a relationship terminated by death can extend beyond the physical world.

The first holiday season after Mom's passing, the family missed her presence and traditions. We were all sad that this December she wouldn't be working late into the nights stitching quilts for the adults and Raggedy Ann and Andy dolls for the younger set, or be caught molding tomato aspic for dinner or performing a homespun duet with Luciano Pavorotti. Since none of us wanted to face a holiday at home without Mom, we arranged to spend Christmas at a cottage on the Oregon coast, hoping the roar of the ocean would distract us in this season of memories.

Two weeks before our trip to Oregon, Hallmark Hall of Fame featured a TV special, *To Dance with the White Dog*, starring Jessica Tandy and Hume Cronyn. A devotee of these late celebrities, I called Dad, urging him to watch. After hanging up, I tuned in, mesmerized by the story about a relationship between a man and woman that is suddenly severed by her death, after which the anguished widower is visited by a white dog, seemingly a manifestation of his wife. As soon as the film ended, Dad called, mumbling through his tears, "Honey, that was wonderful, very tender. Thanks for calling."

During the family Christmas dinner in Oregon, there was a scratch at the window, and a grandchild hollered, "Look! We have a visitor!" Lo and behold, my sister-in-law Kelly opened the door, whereupon a white German shepherd bounded past the desserts arranged on a window seat and began roaming from person to person, nuzzling each one. My dad and I stared at each other in disbelief.

After receiving pats from all, the white dog trotted back out through the entryway, never to reappear during our holiday. Nor did locals remember ever having encountered such an animal. However, the dog's sudden appearance and affectionate behavior convinced Dad and I that we had somehow connected with Mom's spirit and witnessed a mystery of life.

If you have trouble explaining mysterious events that seem to follow a death in the family . . .

In the linear twenty-first century, many of us have traded mystery for science. If we can't experience occurrences with at least one of our senses, we tend to dismiss them—until there are too many coincidences to ignore, at which point we call them "synchronistic events" and consider them meaningful without being defined. Accepting mysteries in life inspires trust in the inexplicable, anticipation of miracles, and an awareness that in the search for airtight explanations you can easily miss the gift.

To prepare for any mysterious experience that may occur in connection with the death of a parent, contemplate these questions:

- How do you explain the imperceptible connections that seem to piece together the tapestry of your existence?
- Can you accept mysteries in life or do you need rational explanations for the phenomena that occur?
- Have you or anyone close to you ever had a mystical experience following the death of a loved one? If so, what do you make of it?

——— COMING OF AGE PASSAGE ———
Holding fate and coincidence in the same palm

202 —— COMING OF AGE

Memorial on the Links

Every death has its own unique style.

Two weeks into my father's stay at Shangri-la, the nearby adult family home, we were notified that the facility would not be able to keep him since he was too disruptive. Already Dad had declared he would never live with us, so it was time to hit the streets again, in search of a new facility within the allotted thirty days. Now the tables were turned: instead of looking for a home with a good inspection record, we had to seek out one willing to take a parent with a bad record.

Eight days later, the owner of Shangri-la called to alert us that Dad had undergone some changes. Arriving within minutes, we encountered two fire engines and an ambulance. Racing up the steps of the home, my heart in my throat, I wondered if Dad was even alive.

As I approached his bed, I realized he could not speak. The owner whispered, "When he opened his eyes a moment ago, it seemed like he'd had a stroke. He sent me a message though. Lifting his 'good' arm, he formed a circle with his thumb and fore-finger, as if to signal, 'right on.' I think he's ready to bid this ole earth good-bye, do you?"

The EMT unit had begun taking Dad's blood pressure and providing oxygen, evidently preparing him for a trip to the hospital. Turning on the owner, I roared, "Why did you call 911? We told you he wanted no heroic measures taken if he wound up like this."

A true professional, she explained, "In a facility, you are required by law to request emergency treatment, Gail. We didn't have a choice."

My next line of attack was the firemen. "Hold it," I said. "He doesn't want to be in any hospital."

An employee responded, "Well, once we're called we need to admit him to a hospital. Sacred Heart is the closest. Why don't you follow the ambulance so you can be with him after he's admitted?"

In near shock myself, I entrusted John with the drive to the ER, where we waited until an assessment of Dad's status was complete. Finally, a physician appeared and announced, "It doesn't look good. He could go at any point or last many days."

Not hesitating, I said, "We're taking him home."

The kind doctor replied, "I'll call hospice. You should be out of here within the hour."

We followed the ambulance again, this time to our home. As the paramedic and emergency medical technician unloaded Dad, I told them, "We want him on the second floor—in our room, so we can sleep with him." Moments later, Dad was propped up in our bedroom, surrounded by family pictures, including one of him at age four, and a hospice team composed of Jane, Shari, and Jim.

Jim, a nurse, devised a communication system whereby Dad could answer our questions by altering his breathing: a long exhalation meaning "no," a short inhalation signifying "yes." Believing Dad was fully impaired, we previously had no idea it was possible to still "speak" with him. Jim also bathed Dad, shaved him, and taught us to interpret signals that he was ready for more morphine.

Kip and Bev arrived within hours of Dad's stroke, contributing to the cocoon of support that enveloped him. Kip took over the management of Dad's pain, while Bev choreographed the household tasks. That night John and I slept, for the first time ever, in the same bedroom with my father, falling into the rhythm of his faint yet regular breathing.

The next day, Saturday, we were wakened by a phone call from Greg and Patti, who said they were en route with three-week-old Jonas, coming to meet his great-grandfather. When they arrived, they carefully handed Jonas to Dad. Placing his palm under the baby's tiny buttocks, with Greg's support Dad raised his great-grandson toward the heavens.

On Sunday, while rotating our vigil among family members, we greeted close friends who came to express love and say good-bye. Our next-door neighbor had gone to the library and checked out audiocassettes of Dad's favorite music, which we played softly (although later we learned from music thanatologists that hearing familiar music can make it more difficult for a person to let go of life).

Monday morning after breakfast, Greg went upstairs for a diaper and heard Dad struggling to breathe. Greg called out to me, but by the time I had run upstairs Dad was gone. I cradled his head, dotted in perspiration, to my chest, his last breath still hanging in the air—a merciful finale.

Our mourning began, replete with insights into the final moments of life. For one, I was challenged by the belief that each person chooses their own way to leave the family. Mom, I reasoned, could have "snuck out" when we were all momentarily away from her bedside. Had Dad tried to do the same but been foiled by the dash for a diaper? Then, too, even though our family felt Dad had been preparing to die during the last months, I now knew it is impossible to be really prepared for someone's passing. In helping me adapt to my absence at the moment of Dad's death, Shari explained that most likely he had already transitioned to a realm beyond and had no need for human connection. Understanding this perspective helped me overcome selfish impulses to call Dad back and thereby risk inhibiting his passage.

Although cultivating intimacy in the final moments of a loved one's life is viewed as ideal in our culture, each individual's circumstances must be honored as a larger and more pragmatic truth. In some instances, such as mine, a family member can be inadvertently preoccupied. In others, a family member can stay away for good reason—as did our daughter Kaaren, who was eight and a half months pregnant and separated from us by more than a thousand miles. As tempting as it may be to judge a family member's absence at such an important time, doing so fails to account for the intimacy that transcends physicality and violates the spirit of grieving.

Two months after Dad's death, we gathered close family and friends in a celebration of his life, at a local golf course. In accordance with Dad's wishes, we played a round of golf, each gripping a paper cup full of Dad's ashes to be spread throughout the eighteen holes. My brothers had designed the event and placed Dad's original clubs at selected holes with instructions for their use. Awards were given to people making the most unusual shot or using the most profanity. Even today when we are all together, we hit the links–in Dad's company.

Dad's journey concluded days after meeting Jonas and weeks before the birth of his first great-granddaughter, Ava. It is soothing to think that somewhere in the seamless realms between the spiritual world and the physical one, they all shared a wink or hug with one another–and that these newest family members carry a profound imprint of Dad's life and wisdom.

If you have the opportunity to anticipate your parent's death . . .

Anticipating a parent's death hypothetically can help prepare you for the actual event, but it is only when you sense finality that you can know the impact their death will have on your spirit, mind, and body. As you imagine or deal directly with a parent's death, consider the following questions:

- Do you need to move closer to your departing parent? Do you understand the reasons for your decision?

- What closure do you need with yourself, your family, or your parent as their time of death approaches?

- Does focusing on the responses of other family members distract you from your own grieving? How might you blend their needs with your own?

- How might you integrate your parent's needs with your own?
- Are you familiar with the resources offered by hospice palliative care? Have you considered enrolling your parent in hospice if your parent is willing and appears to have less than six months to live?

———— COMING OF AGE PASSAGE ————

Staying present to yourself while honoring others

Introducing the ABCs of Mortality

Even if you have laid the foundation by modeling eldercare, don't assume your offspring or young relatives will jump at the chance to deal with your own end-of-life wishes.

Dad's death ended our twelve years in eldercare. Sporadic sunlight permeated my cloud cover of grief, as I trusted I would eventually be restored. Sometimes I felt like an orphan; at other times I marveled at how steadily life goes on.

Weeks later, our kids and their families arrived for a summer holiday. Well briefed in lessons of mortality and newly aware of our own, we felt the urge to bring it up on the last day of their visit.

John broached the subject, saying, "Hey, kids—here we are at a juncture. You know, G. G., Papa, Grandpa, and Grandma are gone now. Maybe you've noticed your old parents getting a little ragged around the edges themselves. Like it or not, you'll be facing some of the same issues we dealt with. Your mom and I think it would be good to talk about these things, like what our final wishes are—should anything happen to us. Then you'll know what to do."

"About what?" our son asked.

I said, "Well, like what our desires would be if we could no longer live at home, or if our quality of life diminished so much that we might not want to go on living."

John raised the ante. "For instance, if we'd suffocate without the aid of a respirator, would we want one? Or if we were starving, would we consent to a feeding tube? And what do we want done with our bodies after we're cremated? Or if one of us dies and the other gets remarried, are there items you would like to have passed on to you rather than given to your new mother or father—or their kids? Or what should you do with the dog if we die? Then, too, you ought to know our plans for your meager inheritance."

A stillness held our group hostage. Realizing this was not going well, John struggled to lighten the topic. "Or hey—what if we'd like to be mummified?"

Our daughter, tiny rivers spilling down her cheeks, bellowed, "I don't want to talk about this stuff!"

Despite empathizing, I was puzzled. Was this the same self-sufficient young woman who had climbed Mount Kilimanjaro, driven to Canada the day after getting her driver's license, and played the role of family confronter for nearly her entire thirty-one years? I spoke softly, "Of course this is hard, darling. But we'll have to talk about it sometime. We don't want you to have to do all the guessing we did."

"I know," she gasped, covering her ears. "But not now!"

Mindful the children had witnessed our journey with their grandparents, we had assumed they would welcome our sharing with enthusiasm, even relief; but deafened by logic, we had misjudged the emotional dimension of the topic. Standing back, we had to acknowledge, much to our dismay, that our children were not the least bit eager to receive the information about us that we wished we had been told by our parents. We had plowed right in without following their lead or getting their permission.

We agreed to revisit the conversation later. If we took our lead feet off the gas before introducing our greatest concerns, they would, we felt, show us the way. Silence reigned for several minutes, then our daughter-in-law said, "Anybody up for one last board game?" As we clambered toward Scrabble, it was clear a new cycle had begun.

If your children or young relatives are not yet ready to consider your mortality . . .

Talking about the inevitable with adult children not yet ready to grapple with their parents' humanity, or with relatives unprepared to deal with an elder's, is an exercise in trial and error. The presentation is never fully acceptable; the timing never quite right. Still raw with grief, we had failed to apply the wisdom gleaned from all our years in eldercare: take a step, stand back, evaluate in order to verify or dismantle, and never get too invested in the outcome.

Unless they suspect you are in a healthcare crisis, your offspring or young relatives might send you roses for initiating such a tough talk, but more likely they will demand a moratorium on the subject. If they do, set a generous deadline for dialogue. Trying to approach such a highly charged discussion too soon or cram it into a short weekend is self-sabotage. Allow ample opportunity for reflection. Before such a discussion suggest that in the interim they do some fieldwork, reading up on end-of-life issues, talking to friends about them, and thinking about the practicalities involved.

While setting the stage for discussing end-of-life issues with adult children or young relatives, consider these questions:

- To maximize receptivity, how might you prepare your children or relatives to learn about your final wishes?

- Keeping your children's or relatives' individual sensitivities in mind, what is the best approach for sharing your final wishes with them?

- Would you feel comfortable recording your wishes for safe-keeping in the event some or all of your children or relatives refuse to discuss them or keep putting you off?

——— COMING OF AGE PASSAGE ———
Accepting your own mortality

APPENDIX A
Parent Questionnaire

Information is the most important tool in all aspects of eldercare. Though there is no way to control future circumstances, gathering information from your parents ahead of time can at least give you a welcome sense of control when they arise. It is therefore wise to discuss possible end-of-life events with your parents when they are physically capable and mentally and emotionally willing, preferably while in their late fifties. Sensitivity is required in initiating these conversations so as not to appear as though you are meddling in their lives or wanting them to die.

A secondary benefit of such conversations is that they help you serve as both a facilitator and educator, enlisting the support of professionals while also providing your parents with pertinent facts and linking them to peers who have had similar healthcare experiences. Diagramming or illustrating certain procedures may at times be necessary as well. Regardless of the educational role you end up playing, be wary of feigned understanding on a parent's part. A nodding head does not connote comprehension but rather signifies the need for you to ask for paraphrasing.

During discussions, issues of control may surface. At such times, although a parent may be grateful for the opportunity to talk about their health status, plans, and desires, they may become uncooperative or provide only selective information, giving you details they think you want while omitting more critical ones. The ability to think ahead and communicate clearly can prevent these conversations from negatively affecting your relationship with your parent.

End-of-life discussions can also elicit a host of fears. Many times, a parent will articulate alarm about becoming a burden, forfeiting control of their life, outliving their money, losing a spouse or partner, being the last of their friends to die, or suffering a prolonged death. When you think your parent is afraid, take a full breath and listen carefully; then, letting go of any agenda you may have had, convey your understanding.

Ultimately, end-of-life discussions provide a source of comfort, ensuring both you and your loved ones that their final days will be dignified and their last wishes honored. If you are lucky, your parents will feel comfortable fully sharing their concerns and desires with you in advance. If they are ill at ease, however, you might explain the advantages of addressing these issues now rather than later. Funerals alone, you could point out, require discussion. They are as much for the living as for respecting the wishes of the deceased since the time survivors spend alone with a loved one's corpse can be very healing. And because funerals are extremely costly it is best to talk about them beforehand rather than when the family is overwhelmed with grief. If your parent still objects, you will have to proceed with little or no direct information.

To gather useful information concerning each parent's current status and future wishes, customize the following parent questionnaire. Part I is designed to help you obtain a general profile that can be updated as time passes. Parts II and III, end-of-life planning geared to pre- and post-death considerations, are divided into three levels of inquiry: Level One questions are generic and can be asked of any parent, Level Two questions are for parents willing to disclose more-than-usual candor, and Level Three questions are aimed at those prepared for soul-searching and personal growth.

As you ask each parent these questions, allow their answers to lead to further inquiries. Take notes for future reference. And remember, no matter how much information you acquire, expect to do some second-guessing while mired in an eldercare crisis.

I. General Profile

Personal Values

How important to you is each of the following? (Rate every item on a scale of 1 to 10, with "1" signifying the least important and "10" the most important.)

- [ ] Making decisions for yourself
- [ ] Staying physically active
- [ ] Residing at your home
- [ ] Sustaining your financial base
- [ ] Participating in hobbies and recreation
- [ ] Spending time with the family
- [ ] Continuing to drive your car
- [ ] Nourishing a rich spiritual base
- [ ] Leaving an inheritance
- [ ] Maintaining intellectual agility
- [ ] Preserving emotional stability
- [ ] Continuing to learn and grow
- [ ] Keeping socially active
- [ ] Retaining a positive physical appearance
- [ ] Having privacy
- [ ] Avoiding personal indebtedness or state assistance

Financial and Legal Matters

- ☐ Who are your financial advisors? (Please provide names, addresses, and phone numbers.)

- ☐ Are you concerned about your financial situation? Why?

- ☐ Do you have any debts? To whom? (Please provide names, addresses, and phone numbers.)

- ☐ Have you transferred any assets? To whom? (Please provide names, addresses, and phone numbers.)

- ☐ Which of the following records do you have, and where are they located?

Will

Funeral plans

Arrangement for dispersal of body after death

Birth and marriage certificates

Divorce papers

Veteran's discharge

Powers of attorney

Advance directive for health care (living will)

Community property agreement

Trusts

Driver's license

Medicare ID #

Medicaid ID #

Insurance policies

    Health insurance

    Dental insurance

    Pharmacy plan

    Life insurance

    Long-term care insurance

    Home insurance

    Auto insurance

Social Security card

Checking and savings account registers

Monthly bank statements

Credit card statements

Safe deposit box numbers, locations, and keys

Titles to car, properties, and other assets

Copies of tax returns and W-2 forms

Pension and retirement programs

Statements and certificates of stocks, bonds, and mutual funds

Deeds, mortgages, sales, investments, and other real estate transactions

Health Status

☐ How would you describe your current state of health–physically, mentally, emotionally, and spiritually?

☐ Do you keep a diary about your symptoms—including when they started and how often they occur—and medications?

☐ Are you concerned about any particular symptoms? Have you noticed changes in them lately?

☐ What medical conditions and surgical procedures have you had during your lifetime? When did these occur?

☐ Who is your primary care physician? (Please provide name, address, and phone number.) Does this person also coordinate interventions among your other providers?

☐ What specialists, if any, do you see on a regular basis? (Please provide names, addresses, and phone numbers.)

☐ When was your last checkup or geriatric assessment? When are you due for the next one?

☐ How much do you weigh? Have you lost or gained weight in recent months?

☐ What foods are you allergic or sensitive to?

☐ Who is your health insurance provider and, if applicable, your secondary insurance provider? (Please provide membership numbers, names, addresses, and phone numbers.) Is the coverage adequate? What benefits do you receive from these policies?

☐ Who is your dentist or denturist? (Please provide name, address, and phone number.)

☐ When was your last dental checkup? When is your next appointment?

☐ Who is your dental insurance provider? (Please provide membership number, name, address, and phone number.) Is the coverage adequate? What benefits do you receive from this policy?

☐ What pharmacy do you use? (Please provide name, address, and phone number.)

☐ Do you have a pharmacy insurance plan? (Please provide membership number, name, address, and phone number.) Is the coverage adequate? What benefits do you receive from this policy?

☐ Are you currently taking any medications? What are the dosages and frequencies?

☐ Are there side effects or allergic reactions to your medications? Have you experienced any of these?

☐ Does your primary care physician have a list of all your current medications, including any nonprescription remedies you take regularly? Has your pharmacist reviewed this list for possibly risky interactions?

☐ How did your parents die? What chronic conditions, if any, did they have over the course of their lives?

☐ Have you suffered any losses that are still weighing heavily on you? How do you actively cope with them?

☐ Do you have concerns about your safety?

☐ Do you sometimes feel lonely? Would you like to interact with more people on a daily basis?

II. Pre-Death Planning

Medical Treatment

Level One

☐ If a healthcare provider gives me a medical diagnosis for you, would you like me to share it with you? Do you want to know the prognosis as well?

☐ If there's any information about your health status that you don't want to know about, will you tell me? If you're unable to speak, how will you signal this information?

☐ If an emergency arises and your primary care physician is unavailable, is there another physician you would agree to see? (Please provide name, address, and phone number.)

☐ What is your preferred hospital? (Please provide name, address, and emergency room phone number.)

Levels Two and Three

☐ Francis Bacon, the early seventeenth-century English philosopher, spoke of "a good death." How would you describe a good death for yourself?

☐ How would you feel about being kept alive on a respirator, and what would it mean to you? For instance, if you were in a coma with no chance of recovery, what would be your treatment of choice? What treatment would you want if you were in a coma with a slight chance of regaining consciousness?

☐ What would be your preferred treatment if you get a disease that can be cured? That can't be cured?

☐ If you have an incurable condition, would you like to be treated for subsequent reversible illnesses you experience?

☐ Under what circumstances would you want diagnostic testing? Does it matter how invasive these tests are?

☐ Would incontinence or impotence be an acceptable side effect of measures taken to extend your life?

☐ How much pain are you willing to endure?

☐ How much helplessness are you willing to experience?

☐ If you do not want extraordinary treatment or heroic measures, how do you define these terms?

☐ Under what circumstances would you want life-sustaining measures withdrawn? Not withdrawn?

☐ In the event you could suffocate without the aid of a respirator, when would you want a respirator? Not want a respirator?

☐ In the event you could starve to death, when would you want a feeding tube? Not want a feeding tube?

☐ When would you want CPR—cardiopulmonary resuscitation, which effectively restarts the heart and breathing following heart and pulmonary failure? Not want it?

☐ If you get sick or have an accident, what kind of medical care do you want?

☐ If you suffer irreversible brain damage, what are your wishes?

☐ If you have a chronic illness, would you want lifesaving surgery after suffering a new health crisis, such as a heart attack?

☐ Under what circumstances should 911 be called? If you are unconscious? If you are undergoing a cardiac arrest? If you are experiencing acute bodily pain?

☐ In the event you need emergency support and your power of attorney is not available, who should be called? If no family members are accessible, who should be contacted?

☐ Would you like to be at home when you die? Under what conditions, if any, would you not want to be at home?

☐ If you are not a hospice client, would you like your physician to serve as an adviser as you die?

☐ Would you otherwise prefer to be alone when you die? If not, whom would you like with you?

Support Services

Level One

☐ In the event of a debilitating illness or accident, would you want the services of a home health agency?

☐ If you are diagnosed with a terminal condition, would you like to see if you qualify for assistance from hospice?

☐ If you require a home health aide, would you prefer a male or female? A nonsmoker? Someone quiet as opposed to chatty? What other criteria are important to you?

Level Two

☐ How do you feel about family members assuming some responsibility for your care—particularly personal care, such as bathing or catheter changes? Is there any function you would not like family members to perform?

☐ If you are in a nursing facility, would you enjoy visits from friends and relatives? Under what circumstances? Is there anyone you do not want to see?

III. Post-Death Considerations

Disposal of the Body

Level One

☐ Have you indicated a desire to be an organ, tissue, or whole body donor either on your driver's license or by securing a federal organ/tissue donor card and giving a duplicate to a family member? (For information, see http://www.organdonor.gov)

☐ Will you be buried or cremated?

☐ How soon after death do you want your body disposed of?

☐ Are you a member of a memorial society? (Please provide name, address, and phone number.)

☐ Have you chosen a cemetery? A plot? If it is a family plot, with whom do you wish to be buried? (Please provide name, address, phone number, and plot number.)

☐ Would you like to have an open casket? A viewing of the body? Display of an urn?

☐ Would you like any bathing, cosmetology, or restorative procedures undertaken by professionals or others?

☐ If you will be buried, would you like a grave liner or a vault? Are there particular articles of clothing or jewelry you would like to wear? Items you want buried with you?

☐ If you will be cremated, what would you like done with your ashes? Do you want them placed in an urn and buried? Placed in an urn and transported to a columbrian? Scattered?

☐ If you are a navy veteran or have made special arrangements through the Environmental Protection Agency, do you want to be buried at sea?

☐ If you die before stating your choices for disposal of the body, who should make these decisions for you?

Level Two

☐ If you live in a state that permits burial in a family's backyard, would this be your preferred choice? (For information, call the national or state Funeral Directors Association.)

☐ If permitted, would you like your pet to be buried in your plot?

Level Three

☐ If your state permits families to care for their own dead, would this be your preference? (For information, call the national or state Funeral Directors Association.)

The Funeral, Memorial, or Commemoration

Level One

☐ Have you made arrangements with a funeral home? (Please provide name, address, and phone number.)

☐ Have these arrangements been paid for?

☐ Do you want a graveside service? A processional?

☐ If you have a service, who should preside or officiate? Is there any special message you would like them to deliver from you?

☐ Would you like any particular music (or musicians), scriptural readings, photography, art, memories, or words of your own included in a commemoration event?

Level Two

☐ Have you made alternative arrangements in the event you die in the vicinity of a second residence?

☐ Would you like a religious or nonreligious service? Private or public?

☐ Do you want a grave marker or headstone? What would you like engraved on it? Have you arranged for this?

☐ Are there any particular family rituals you would like observed after you die?

☐ Would you like to write your own obituary (free public announcement in the newspaper)? If not, who should write one and what would you like mentioned in it? Have you selected an accompanying photograph?

☐ Who should write your death notice (paid listing in the newspaper) if the family decides to submit one?

☐ If you are a veteran, would you like to have a casket draped with an American flag? A veteran's cemetery marker?

Level Three

☐ If you have a service, who should give the eulogy? Is there anything you would especially like them to say?

☐ If you become terminally ill, would you prefer to have a ceremony before you die so you can attend it?

☐ If you have a processional, who should ride in the hearse? Is there any order in which you would like others to follow?

☐ If you will be buried, who should serve as pallbearers? Ushers?

☐ Do you wish to have an autopsy if there is a choice?

☐ Who do you perceive as your immediate family?

☐ Which of your friends, colleagues, and workplace associates should be notified regarding your death? (Please provide names and phone numbers.)

☐ Do you have a preference for the expression of condolences, such as donations to specific charities? Do you wish to designate a memorial?

Tip: A parent's request for no service or memorial can be at odds with the survivors' needs to gain closure. To circumvent the potential for difficulties, exercise your creativity. For instance, following her mother's death one woman had a ceremony for herself, inviting a close circle of friends to come support her in this transition.

Distribution of Belongings

<u>Level One</u>

☐ What possessions would you like given to others after your death? Which don't matter?

☐ What should happen with your clothing?

☐ Do you have any idea of the value of your possessions? Would you like items to be divided equally? If so, what does *equally* mean to you?

☐ Would you like to decide who gets specific items? Would you prefer the family decides during a discussion?

☐ If you don't care how your belongings are distributed, who should be responsible for deciding?

<u>Level Two</u>

☐ If the family makes choices about the items in your estate, would you like your children to have priority over your grandchildren?

☐ If heirlooms are given to family members, should they have the right to sell them? Would you rather have them kept in the family?

Level Three

☐ If one of your children dies, should their partner make decisions about what to do with the items inherited from you? Should these items be passed on to other blood-related children or grandchildren?

☐ What would you like to have done with your pet?

Tip: Although your parent might prefer to verbally express how worldly goods are distributed after they die, writing down their wishes will prevent later confusion among family members.

Parents who are unable or unwilling to provide the information necessary to complete this questionnaire up the ante for any family member wishing to act on their behalf. If your parent is physically unable to furnish answers, then as health issues arise you will have to rely on knowledge gleaned from your own memories, stories recounted by relatives, or other wellsprings of information about your parent's values. You might uncover more details by talking to their friends or going through a memorabilia box or photograph album.

Once you have culled information, facilitate a round-robin discussion among family members to collectively figure out how best to proceed. Fathoming the unknown often begins with articulating the known. With this in mind, consider opening your discussion with a phrase like "If I were Mom (Dad) in this situation, I would probably want to . . ." Listen for comments such as "Well, Mom never did have confidence in doctors" or "Dad always said we'd have to dynamite him out of his house."

On the other hand, if your parent refuses to share information, this actually constitutes a decision. Perhaps the most you can do in such a situation is say to yourself, "Since Dad (Mom) refused to talk about these issues, I am going to interpret that he (she) is leaving them up to my better judgment." The message to convey is that there's no need for self-incrimination in the future. Toward this end, before implementing any course of action make sure you can answer the following question in the affirmative: "Knowing what I do about my parent, is my decision framed in accordance with the greatest good possible?"

Also consider seeking opinions from other "interpreters," like family members, friends, clergy, elderlaw attorneys, family physicians, geriatric care managers, case managers, personal care aides, home health providers, counselors or psychotherapists, volunteers, and service personnel, such as postal or newspaper delivery workers. As a last resort, especially if family members are disagreeable or threatening to intervene, appeal to appropriate agencies for support, including your local Area Agency on Aging or Adult Protective Services.

APPENDIX B
A Family Meeting Model

When a parent needs care, a family meeting of all immediate members can provide an ideal forum for creating a plan that is respectful, compassionate, and realistic. Subsequent meetings may be arranged as needed, especially if the parent's health status has changed, a crisis is escalating, or stronger collaboration is required. In advance of each family meeting, it is vital that all participants have the same information and access to one another. If gathering at a central location is impossible due to geographic separation, schedule a telephone conference with follow-up mail or e-mail networking.

The parent, if interested, should be encouraged to take part so they can express their needs and desires directly. If they do not want to attend or if their presence is apt to pose significant obstacles, family members can meet without them. In the interest of harmony, however, an absentee parent should be informed of the meeting in advance and told about outcomes afterward. If they have not already sought the advice of professionals, such as an elderlaw attorney and financial adviser, they might also be asked to confer with experts who can serve as family consultants after death.

The following model for a family meeting contains elements essential to eldercare and is geared specifically to a first-time gathering. Vary the guidelines to suit your family's situation, remembering that the goal of your meeting is to overcome differences well enough to work as a family team in caring for your ailing parent.

Preparations

- Consult with your parent's primary care physician about any recent changes in your parent's health status.
- Update family members, relaying the doctor's report and your own observations of your parent's situation.

- Encourage family members to research relevant conditions and aging in general.

Procedure

- Welcome the assembled participants, offering sincere words of celebration about the family's willingness to collabrate in the best interest of their parent by drawing upon their individual strengths.
- Designate a recorder to take minutes and a leader, or coleaders, to facilitate the meeting. The leader then sets the tone by acknowledging the impact of eldercare on the entire family.
- Develop an agenda and a commitment to stick to it.
- Ask participants to agree on a problem-solving philosophy, such as deferring to the parent's stated needs or, if your parent is incapable of making good judgments, to their spouse, offspring, or next of kin.
- Set meeting goals and a timeline.
- Establish communication guidelines, such as the following:
  1. These meetings are not for airing unfinished business. Old conflicts are best resolved outside of the meetings.
  2. Here we voice only our own opinions and speak only of our own experiences, saying, for example, "The way I see it is . . ." instead of "Many of us in the room feel . . . ," or "I felt uncomfortable when you said . . ." rather than "You made me feel guilty when . . ."
  3. No family member will cancel participation in parent care without first sharing their decision with the team.
- Determine a decision-making style. Generally, consensus is the best option. However, in the event of ongoing discord among family members, you may need to resort to a

"majority rules" model or delegate decision making to an ad hoc task force.

- Identify immediate caretaking challenges and describe what might happen if nothing is done.

- Brainstorm solutions and arrive at decisions.

- Ask if anyone is withholding an opinion or concern.

- Make a plan based on your decisions. Incorporate hands-on care, as well as fact finding and information gathering.

- Assign tasks to the family team, giving special attention to the following considerations:

  1. Resolve whether professionals in your group will serve also as resources—a second-best option since it is difficult to remain emotionally uninvolved—or if the group will seek outside counsel on medical, financial, and legal issues.

  2. Use the inventory of eldercare tasks listed in Appendix E, pages 243–246, as a prototype, tailoring it where needed to suit your parent's needs.

  3. Determine who will be the primary caregiver or caregivers. If the care distribution among family members is disproportionate, consider compensating key caregivers in some way.

- Create a beginning budget, if appropriate.

- Evaluate the meeting, amending the plan if necessary.

- If desired, enlarge the team to encompass particular experts for assisting the caregivers.

- Record and distribute information for a telephone tree, if needed.

- Schedule mutually agreeable dates, times, and locations for future meetings.

- Celebrate the cooperative spirit among you that has emerged to deal with adversity. Perhaps organize a potluck featuring family recipes from earlier days, or arrange to pore over photograph albums together or to meet at sunset for storytelling.

Tip: If your family is not ready to handle such a meeting objectively, consider bringing in a skilled facilitator such as a counselor, geriatric care manager, agency caseworker, or member of the clergy.

Ten Commandments for Working in Harmony

1. Honor thy family culture. If your family is new to intimacy, accommodate the lack of expertise in conflict management and emotional resolution.

a. Before coming together, identify relationship aspects in need of groundwork. At the family meeting, unaccusingly bring forward these observations, not for problem-solving purposes but to begin formulating an honest, mutually recognizable database. This guideline pertains specifically to extremely diverse families inexperienced in direct communication.

b. Acknowledge unhealthy patterns prevalent in family communication, such as diverting conflict or refusing to accept the existence of problems. Once recognized openly, such nonproductive group behaviors can gradually change to bring about preferred outcomes. Though major shifts may not occur during eldercare tenure, the small alterations that unfold can form new building blocks for the future.

c. Warn team members before taking an unorthodox approach, saying, for example, "I know that in our family we usually don't deal with each other directly but rather air our grievances through another family member. I think in this situation, we need to do something different, and I propose _____."

d. If your parent resists active participation in these discussions, ask them to engage for the sake of their children or use methods of gentle persuasion such as telling a story about what happened when people in another family didn't talk. There are many tales about parents who, refusing to disclose financial information, die leaving their kin hunting and pecking for general details about investments, or praying a mail carrier will deliver an annual report substantiating assets.

2. Clarify interpretations. Elucidate the group's understanding of various exigencies. For instance, if your parent has said, "Absolutely no life support," and the group believes that with life support there is hope for a recovery involving quality of life, to overcome potential conflict take time to compare your parent's definition of quality of life with the group's definition. Vast discrepancies in understanding, if left unresolved, can sabotage progress.

3. Share the responsibility for confronting difficulties. If all "heavy lifting" is left to the group leader, other members miss the opportunity to develop these essential skills. Also, the group may soon expect the leader to be the confronter in all future encounters—a dynamic that increases the risk of scapegoating or of individuals' decreased investment in outcomes. Ideally, group members play many roles.

4. Notice each individual's body language and other nonverbal cues. These often unconscious responses may reveal more about the effectiveness of a conversation than words themselves. Is someone being silent and gritting their teeth, or fidgeting? What might this mean? In such instances you could ask, "Is there something you would like to add to the discussion?"

5. Thou shalt not judge or blame. To refrain from evaluating others' opinions or motives is to lower the potential for defensiveness within the group. Also abstain from accusatory remarks such as "You always make me feel . . ." and "Here we go again—you are constantly criticizing . . ." Meetings conducted free of censure invite participants to focus on the common goal and troubleshoot cooperatively.

6. *Thou shalt not form alliances or triangles.* Group settings increase the potential for odd-man-out scenarios or contestual encounters, both of which are counterproductive. Affirm everyone's right to their unique opinion and its importance in negotiating the path ahead.

7. *Void the idea of perfection.* The most important conversations might feel awkward, tactless, bungling—anything but perfect. To achieve progress as a team, each family member needs to be respected for their style of communication and beliefs about successful solutions.

8. *Allow.* Be willing to let family meetings unfold spontaneously within the structure you have created. Learn when to speak and when to listen. Giving voice to touchy issues welcomes them into your forum so they can be addressed. But if a member just needs to feel understood in order to move forward, allow instead for attentive listening.

9. *Instead of giving up, give over.* Don't be disheartened by intense or angry coversations, for they can lead to closer ties. But if there is no way to reach common ground and your interactions are causing more damage than good, be willing to defer decisions to a recognized legal appointee such as a power of attorney.

10. *Revisit your conversations.* After the meeting, check in intermittently with other team members to see if everyone is still on the same wavelength. It is common to have second thoughts or new insights as time passes, or to undergo a change of heart or circumstances. Teams that stay updated avoid needless surprises and reconvene with ongoing rapport.

Dependency Continuum for Aging Adults

The diagram below delineates a continuum of increasingly special-ized housing and service options from which aging adults may ben-efit as they progress from independent to dependent living. While some move slowly through these sequences, others plummet rapidly toward dependence and the need for enhanced assistance. Several of these options are financed by government aid for elders who qualify.

Housing		*Services*
At home	**INDEPENDENCE**	Information, referrals, assistance
Shared living		Financial and legal counseling
Senior apartment		Senior centers
Accessory apartment		
Live-in companion		Housekeeping and shopping
Active adult community		Transportation
Elder cottage housing		Companionship services
Subsidized housing		Case management
Retirement community		
Continuing care retirement community		Assistive equipment
		Emergency response system
Assisted living		Home-delivered meals
Adult foster home		
Catered living		Support groups
Rehabilitation facility		Home care and home health
Nursing home or skilled nursing facility	**DEPENDENCE**	Rehabilitative therapy
Memory care unit or Alzheimer's wing		Adult protective services
		Adult day care or day health
Hospital room (terminal stage)		Hospital care
Hospice house		Hospice care

233

APPENDIX D

Eldercare Resources

Caregiver Support

ARCH National Respite Network
800-473-1727
www.respitelocator.org
The National Respite Locator Service, helping caregivers of people with chronic or terminal illness find respite services locally or while traveling or relocating

Children of Aging Parents (CAPS)
800-227-7294
www.caps4caregivers.org
A membership organization offering adult children high-quality reliable information, referrals, support, and advocacy

Eldercare Locator
800-677-1116
www.eldercare.gov
A service providing details about the nearest Area Agency on Aging, as well as state information and referral services

ElderWeb
www.elderweb.com
An online research site furnishing links to eldercare housing, financial, medical, and legal resources; policies and statistics; and help in locating lost records

Family Caregiver Alliance
800-445-8106
www.caregiver.org
An organization featuring a wide array of need-based services

for families and friends who provide the elderly with long-term care at home

Medicare

www.medicare.gov

An online source listing Medicare and supplemental programs by state and county, while also supplying quality and inspection information on Medicare-certified nursing homes

National Alliance for Caregiving

415-434-3388

www.caregiving.org

A group that conducts research, develops national projects, and increases public awareness of important family caregiving issues

National Association of Geriatric Care Managers

520-881-8008

www.caremanager.org

A source for locating geriatric care managers in regions nationwide

The National Family Caregivers Association

800-896-3650

www.nfcacares.org

A membership organization providing caregivers with information, education, support, public awareness, and advocacy

Visiting Nurse Associations of America (VNAA)

617-737-3200

www.vnaa.org

An organization furnishing compassionate, high-quality, and cost-effective home care to individuals in need of nursing services

Housing Options

American Association of Homes and Services for the Aging (AAHSA)

202-783-2242

www.aahsa.org

An organization providing housing information based on its membership of more than 5,600 not-for-profit nursing homes, continuing care retirement communities, as well as assisted living and senior housing facilities

Assisted Living Federation of America (ALFA)

703-691-8100

www.alfa.org

An online source that helps locate assisted living facilities

A Place for Mom

877-666-3239

www.aplaceformom.com

A free advisory service for families in search of eldercare

Financial Advice

National Association of Insurance Commissioners

816-842-3600

www.naic.org

A consumer-based organization dedicated to the fair and equitable treatment of insurance shoppers and offering a free "Shopper's Guide to Long-Term Care Insurance"

National Association of Personal Financial Advisors

888-366-2732

www.napfa.org

A referral service to fee-only local planners who receive no commissions on sales of financial products

Legal Aid

AARP

888-687-2277

www.aarp.org/legalsolutions/legalglossary.html

A membership organization offering a comprehensive online legal glossary and benefits such as discounts, advocacy, information on aging, advice for living well, and award-winning publications

National Academy of Eldercare Attorneys (NAELA)

520-881-4005

www.naela.com

An organization that assists in locating local attorneys who specialize in elderlaw

Medical Information

Alzheimer's Association

800-272-3900

www.alz.org

American Diabetes Association

800-342-2383

www.diabetes.org

American Heart Association

800-242-8721

www.americanheart.org

American Parkinson's Disease Foundation

800-223-2372

www.apdaparkinson.com

American Prostate Society
410-859-3735
www.ameripros.org

American Stroke Association
888-478-7653
www.strokeassociation.org

Amyotrophic Lateral Sclerosis (ALS, or Lou Gehrig's Disease)
800-782-4747
www.alsa.org

Arthritis Foundation
800-283-7800
www.arthritis.org

Asthma and Allergy Foundation
800-727-8462
www.aafa.org

Cancer Information Services
800-422-6237
www.cancer.gov

Eyecare America: Senior Eye Care Program
800-222-3937
www.eyecareamerica.org

Huntington's Disease Society of America
800-345-4372
www.hdsa.org

Institute of Diabetes, Digestive and Kidney Disease
800-860-8747
www.niddk.hih.gov

Leukemia and Lymphoma Society
800-955-4572
www.leukemia.org

Lupus Foundation of America
800-558-0121
www.lupus.org

National Multiple Sclerosis Society
800-344-4867
www.nmss.org

National Organization for Rare Disorders
800-999-6673
www.rarediseases.org

National Sleep Foundation
202-347-3471
www.sleepfoundation.org

End-of-Life Support

Choice in Dying
800-989-9455
www.partnershipforcaring.org
The inventor of living wills in 1967, this organization fosters communication about complex end-of-life issues.

National Hospice and Palliative Care Organization
800-658-8898
www.nhpco.org
A compassionate team-oriented approach to expert medical care, pain management, and emotional and spiritual support expressly tailored to people facing a life-limiting illness or injury. Support is provided also to their loved ones.

National Institute for Jewish Hospice

800-446-4448

www.nijh.org

A hospice program providing free telephone counseling, referrals, and professional training in helping Jewish people who are terminally ill

Funeral Agencies

Funeral Consumer Alliance

800-765-0107

www.funerals.org

A nonprofit agency protecting consumers' rights to choose a meaningful, dignified, and affordable funeral

National Funeral Directors Association (NFDA)

800-228-6332

www.nfda.org

The largest funeral service organization in the world, and one dedicated to quality assurance

APPENDIX E
Eldercare Tasks

To distribute basic eldercare responsibilities, read this list aloud at your first family meeting or use it as a reference in conversations with team members. In each box, place the initials of people who have agreed to perform the corresponding task.

Personal Care

☐ Meals–preparation, supervision, feeding

☐ Bathing and toileting

☐ Personal hygiene

☐ Dressing and grooming

☐ Hair–scheduling and transport, or in-home care

☐ Laundry and mending

☐ Housekeeping

☐ Shopping–groceries, clothing, personal items, household goods, cleaning supplies

☐ Organizing mail, papers, and correspondence

☐ Creating and maintaining Rolodex

☐ Teaching tasks a departed loved one may have performed

☐ Monitoring driving ability

☐ Providing transportation

☐ Setting up neighborhood support system

☐ Arranging entertainment and recreation

☐ Ensuring fulfillment of spiritual needs

☐ Pet care

☐ Planning special occasions–holidays, visits, vacations

☐ Providing companionship and emotional support

☐ Coordinating respite support

☐ Communicating with other family members about personal care

Health Care

☐ Researching local support systems

☐ Scheduling appointments–routine, therapy, crisis

☐ Accompanying parent to appointments

☐ Ordering and maintaining medical alert equipment

☐ Securing and maintaining special supplies

☐ Preparing and posting emergency information

☐ Medications–purchasing, monitoring, administering

☐ Attending to postsurgical care

☐ Monitoring health–skin, feet, eyesight, hearing, dental, mental

☐ Arranging for exercise and physical therapy

☐ Communicating with healthcare providers

☐ Discussing health care with parent

☐ Communicating with other family members about health care

Housing

☐ Home maintenance–storm windows, screens, roofing, painting

☐ Grounds upkeep–lawn, garden, trees, walkways

☐ Monitoring safety of home environment

☐ Repairs–plumbing, electricity, drains, furnace, hot water heater

☐ Stocking household supplies and managing inventory

☐ Organizing family work parties

☐ Discussing housing needs with parent

☐ Researching alternative living arrangements–respite, emergencies, assisted living, adult family homes, skilled nursing facilities

☐ Moving parent to long-term care facility

☐ Communicating with other family members about housing

Finances

☐ Financial assessment–retirement plan, investments, insurance, income, savings, hidden valuables

☐ Setting up and monitoring monthly budget

☐ Paying bills

☐ Reconciling bank accounts

☐ Reviewing statements–Medicare, Medicaid, medical

☐ Overseeing travel expenses

Purchasing duplicate items—remote controls, keys, eyeglasses, batteries

 Discussing finances with parent

 Communicating with other family members about finances

Legal Matters

 Locating an elderlaw attorney

Ensuring the existence of a will, advance directive for health care, power of attorney, other end-of-life necessities

Organizing safe deposit box

Checking funeral and other post-death arrangements

Discussing legal matters with parent

Communicating with other family members about legal matters

Checking Out Nursing Homes

To decide on a nursing home most likely to meet the needs and preferences of your parent, list recommendations culled from telephone inquiries, feedback from people you trust, newspaper articles, and brochures. Then visit a few facilities, taking along a pad and pen and dropping in unannounced several times—before breakfast, at lunchtime, before dinner, and during the evening—to observe various shifts of workers and their interactions with the residents. While touring each facility, stay out of the way of busy personnel yet remain unrushed and fully aware of everything around you.

Begin by observing the facility and answering the following questions:

- Is the facility clean? (Do the "sniff" test.) Comfortable? Well maintained?
- Is the space conducive to residents' needs? Are there quiet sitting areas to accommodate the desire for intimate conversations or reflection? Is there color coding to give direction where needed? Is the home cheerful? Well lit?
- What is the emotional tenor?
- Do residents look well cared for?
- Is the staff friendly? Courteous and respectful? Attentive? How long do residents wait after signaling for help?
- What happens at mealtime? Are residents in need of feeding assistance given adequate support? Does the staff attempt to engage individuals who seem to be isolating themselves? Is the food fresh, nutritious, and well prepared?
- What types of social activities are offered and encouraged?
- Are residents out of bed? Up and about? Talking with one another?

- Are eyeglasses and teeth clean? Hair combed? Hands and nails scrubbed? Are fingernails and toenails clipped?
- Are there direct private telephone lines in the rooms?
- What does posted information tell you about the facility?
- Do the staff and residents seem to share genuine affection?
- How does the staff handle difficult residents?

To gather more information, interview as many residents as possible, assuring them of confidentiality. If these interviews become emotionally draining, you may have difficulty understanding the residents' answers, in which case request clarification when necessary or repeat the replies you have heard to see if you got them right. Questions to ask include the following:

- What do you like best about living here?
- What would you change if you could?
- What do you hope will never change?

Round out your fact-finding mission by interviewing the administrator and at least one staff member. If necessary, make appointments in advance so you can secure sufficient time to receive answers to the following questions:

- What is your ratio of residents to staff? Does this ratio vary over a twenty-four-hour cycle?
- What levels of care—such as physical therapy, occupational therapy, feeding tubes, beds for extremely overweight residents—are you prepared to offer residents?
- Do you participate with Medicare and Medicaid?
- What are your rates? When do you bill? Do you have payment plans?
- What special services do you offer (barber or hair stylist, laundry)? Is there a fee?

- Do you provide transportation to local events?

- What are your visiting guidelines? How is the family of the resident involved in your program? Do they have twenty-four-hour access to the resident?

- Does the family have access to the staff? The resident's chart?

- If the family has a concern, whom should they alert?

- How is the resident's personal property protected?

- Are there problems with theft?

- How much time is allowed to pass before a resident using their call light is responded to?

- Do the rehabilitative services include a spiritual and psychological focus? How is depression addressed?

- How are people paired who cannot afford a private room? What if someone seems like they would be better off alone?

- If a resident requires hospital admission, will their room be held? For how long?

- Under what conditions might a resident be asked to leave?

Finally, ask to see the latest inspection report and complaint records. While reviewing them, request explanations where necessary.

Share the results of all three surveys with family members and involve them in making the best decision possible regarding your parent's placement; in the event of unresolved controversy, call in a third party. Even after placing your parent in the chosen nursing home, continue your vigilance. If concerns arise, appeal to your local ombudsman, an advocate for nursing home residents, by visiting the Web site www.ltcombudsman.org or www.eldercare.gov, or by calling the Eldercare Locator at 800-677-1116.

APPENDIX G
Rituals for the Journey

The following activities can anchor your eldercare experiences in a coming of age perception of reality. As this perception deepens and solidifies, caretaking, despite unavoidable hardship, gradually transforms into a cause for celebration.

- Keep a diary of your experiences, noting differences you are making in your parent's life. Do this even if you find only three minutes a day to write.

- List positive attributes you have brought to interactions involving disappointment or regret. Consciously add these to your daily itinerary.

- Plant flowers or trees to commemorate your parent and your investment in their care.

- Say a prayer, either silently or with your parent, each time you leave them.

- Visit a quiet space for at least twenty minutes a day to make peace with yourself. Negotiate this time of solitude with immediate family members or housemates. Invest in earplugs if necessary.

- Have lunch at least once a week with someone you cherish.

- Record your dreams. Now that you are drawn back into the fold of family life, your subconscious world may offer you rich imagery to strive for.

- Build a bridge from grief to gratitude. Ask yourself, "What is the loss I feel today?" and "What am I grateful for today?"

- Make a scrapbook of your parent's aphorisms or stories. Or create a library of videotapes, audiotapes, or photograph albums depicting your parent's passage into aging and dying.

- Bring nature into your parent's environment by planting an herb window-garden, arranging a small indoor rockery, or suspending a bird feeder outside their bedroom window.

- Sew a memory quilt decorated with special buttons or articles of clothing from the past, or design a coat-of-arms from family memorabilia.

- Even if you are too tired to lift a book, end each day with an insight distilled from the wisdom of someone who gave themselves completely to life, such as the Lebanese poet Kahlil Gibran, who wrote: "Your joy is your sorrow unmasked. And the selfsame well from which your laughter rises was oftentimes filled with your tears."

Eldercare Glossary

activities of daily living (ADLs). Actions necessary for day-to-day existence, such as feeding, dressing, and grooming oneself

acute care. Medical care provided under the supervision of a physician in a hospital, as opposed to the skilled nursing or intermediate care offered in a nursing home

adult day care (also known as **adult day health**). A facility furnishing social activities, therapies, and personal enrichment to elders who cannot be left alone during the day

adult family homes (also known as **adult foster homes** or **certified family homes**). Private residences licensed to give a small number of occupants (usually between four and six) a variety of services, including room and board, personal care, and sometimes specialized care and skilled nursing

advance directive for health care (also known as **living will, healthcare directive,** or **directive to physicians**). A document describing one's preferences for life-sustaining treatments when diagnosed with a terminal, incurable condition caused by injury or illness and unable to speak for oneself

aging in place. Remaining at home as long as possible and requesting assistance when necessary

Alzheimer's care. Care for people with Alzheimer's disease, ranging from in-home services to assisted living support to full-time skilled nursing care

Area Agencies on Aging (AAA). Local or regional organizations that, established under the Older Americans Act, coordinate and administer a wide variety of services for the elderly

assisted living facility (AL; also known as a **personal care home**). A licensed boarding home offering individual apartments that feature privacy, independence, personal choice, and often such services as meals, personal care, medication assistance, limited supervision, organized activities, and skilled nursing

assistive equipment (also known as **assistive devices**). Equipment designed to help the disabled perform ADLs, such as walkers, lifts, hearing aids, and talking clocks

capitation. Reimbursement to healthcare providers, based on a fixed dollar amount per person per month rather than on a fee-for-service plan

cardiopulmonary resuscitation (CPR). A combination of mouth-to-mouth breathing (or another ventilation technique) and chest compressions, keeping oxygenated blood flowing to the person's brain and vital organs until normal heart action can be restored

caregiver. One who provides services, assistance, or support to a person who is ill or disabled

care management. A "plan of care" for services or treatment based on a professional review of the individual's physical, social, psychological, and health challenges

case management. Assistance, advocacy, and screening used to identify elderly people at risk, assess their needs such as in-home care, and implement coordinated case plans or oversee care services provided by others

catered living. Twenty-four-hour access to a skilled caregiver and a resident services coordinator who see to the unique needs of program participants, including those still living with a spouse or other family member

coinsurance. A copayment made by an individual after their insurer has paid its portion of the bill

community-based services (also known as **community-based care**). Not-for-profit public and private assistance programs offering such services as transportation and shopping

community property agreement. A document allowing married people to avoid probate after death by disposing of their property to the surviving spouse

companionship services. Camaraderie for the elderly, especially the homebound, furnished by volunteers participating in "friendly visitors" or "telephone reassurance" programs or pet-assisted therapy

congregate meals (also known as **senior meals** or **nutrition services**). Group meals prepared for the elderly at local senior or community centers

continuing care retirement communities (CCRCs). Facilities offering a variety of housing arrangements to meet the lifetime needs of residents, including independent living, assisted living, and skilled nursing care

discharge planning. A hospital consultation leading to a convalescing patient's placement in a setting with support services and information about community resources

elder abuse. Neglect (or self-neglect), exploitation, abandonment, or physical mistreatment of an elderly person

eldercare. Assistance provided to seniors in need of physical, social, psychological, financial, or spiritual support

elderhostel. A worldwide educational travel program for people age sixty or older, involving short courses given in colleges, universities, museums, theaters, and national parks

elderlaw attorney. An attorney specializing in legal problems of the elderly

emergency response systems (also known as **medical alert systems**). In-home electronic alarm devices, usually worn as a necklace or bracelet, with signals that can be activated for assistance twenty-four hours a day

employment services. Help for elders and retirees seeking employment opportunities

end-of-life planning. Organizing for the final stages of life, including talking with the family about death, determining the extent to which medical or hospice care is needed, and making financial, legal, funeral, and burial or cremation arrangements

energy assistance and weatherization. A program for low-income seniors needing help with payment of fuel bills and home protection against winter weather

estate planning. The process of preserving one's property and arranging for its transfer after death

financial assistance. Aid available through programs geared to energy assistance, food stamps, prescription drug assistance, and financial counseling

geriatric assessment. Evaluation of all facets of heath and safety needs by a geriatrician and team of specialists

geriatric care manager (GCM). A healthcare professional who assesses the overall situations of elders and creates and oversees a plan for their care

gerontology. Study of the aging process

guardian (also known as **conservator**). A person, appointed by the court, who is responsible for making healthcare decisions and managing assets for an individual found to be legally incapacitated

guardian ad litem. A court-appointed individual chosen to investigate and represent the interests of a person for whom a guardianship has been requested

home care (also known as **personal care services** or **chore services**). Nonmedical assistance provided to ill or injured people at home, including housekeeping, meal preparation, bathing, monitoring of medications, and transportation

home health care. Health-related services furnished by registered nurses (RNs), licensed practical nurses (LPNs), and employees of home healthcare agencies, such as changing wound dressings and providing tube feedings

home modification. Alterations designed to prevent accidents or facilitate activities in households involving people with changing needs due to aging or to declining health

hospice care. Medicare-subsidized care for the terminally ill and their families, emphasizing pain management and control of symptoms, as opposed to curative interventions

independent living unit. Senior housing devoid of specialized services to tenants

intensive care unit (ICU). A hospital unit specially equipped and staffed to provide continuous vital-sign monitoring of seriously ill or postsurgical patients

intermediate-care facility (ICF). A nursing facility providing twenty-four-hour basic medical care to patients needing rehabilitative services but not intravenous therapy or feeding tubes

intestacy. Being without a will, in which case upon the person's death their property passes to heirs in keeping with state statute requirements

legal assistance. Advice and representation for senior citizens engaged in legal matters such as consumer issues, government benefits, and tenant rights

living trust (also known as **revocable living trust**). A document transferring a person's assets into a trust that need not be registered with the courts in probate and can therefore be altered or revoked prior to their death

living will (also known as **directive to physician** or **advance directive for health care**). A document instructing physicians about the desired medical treatment if one is diagnosed with a terminal, incurable condition and has lost the ability to communicate their wishes

long-distance caregiver. A person attending to an elderly individual more than 100 miles away

long-term care facility. An assisted living center or nursing or retirement home providing various healthcare services

long-term care insurance. Privately purchased Medicare supplements (Medigap) as well as nursing home, in-home care, hospital, and personal health insurance to cover other costs

Meals on Wheels (also known as **nutrition services**). A community-based service delivering meals to the homes of elders, preferably for a minimal charge or a donation

Medicaid. A federal and state program paying for health care and long-term care needs of low-income individuals who meet eligibility standards

Medicare. A federal health insurance program designed for Americans age sixty-five or older providing healthcare benefits earned during one's employment

ombudsman. A state employee who advocates on behalf of residents of skilled nursing facilities, boarding homes, and other long-term care facilities to resolve complaints and quality-of-life concerns

outpatient care. Care provided in a medical facility to patients who are not admitted to the hospital for an overnight stay, as opposed to those admitted for twenty-four-hour care

power of attorney (POA). A document giving a designated person the legal authority to act as one's agent

probate. The process whereby the court appoints a personal representative to administer the terms of a deceased person's will

provider. A person or place that outsources medical services, or a supplier of medical equipment

relocation assistance. Help given to elderly people moving from home to a long-term care facility or other new residence

respite care. Temporary care provided by a volunteer or social service agency for purposes of relieving a primary caregiver

senior center. A community-run gathering place featuring meals, structured activities, exercise programs, travel opportunities, and social events for senior citizens

senior housing options. The variety of living quarters available to elders in any area, including retirement communities, assisted living, nursing facilities, government-subsidized housing, and shared housing

skilled nursing facility (SNF). A nursing home providing full-time skilled nursing care, supported by medical equipment or specialty services, to the chronically ill or people recently discharged from a hospital

spend-down. The process by which an elder qualifies for Medicaid benefits by paying for medical and nursing care until their remaining assets have dropped below the state's eligibility limit

subacute care. Care for a patient who, though medically stable, is seriously ill and in need of highly skilled rehabilitative assistance in a nursing home setting

support groups. Networks providing information, emotional sustenance, and companionship to people sharing a common problem or challenge

telephone reassurance. Safety and support measures provided to homebound or disabled individuals through regular telephone contact with trained volunteers

Title VI. Funding for Native American aging programs designed to meet the unique needs of older American Indians, Aleuts, Eskimos, and Hawaiians

transportation and escort. Door-to-door drivers and vehicles available through volunteer groups, and van services for people lacking access to public or private transportation

trust. A form of ownership under which property is held and managed by a designated person or institution for the benefit of other people or institutions

volunteer opportunities. Various means for contributing to the community–activities through which healthy elders extend their vitality

will. A document detailing the post-death disposition of property to specific individuals through an executor or personal representative

Bibliography

Beerman, Susan, and Judith Rappaport-Musson. *Eldercare 911: The Caregiver's Complete Handbook for Making Decisions.* New York: Prometheus Books, 2002.

Byock, Ira. *Dying Well: The Prospect for Growth at the End of Life.* New York: Riverhead Books, 1997.

Harwell, Amy. *Ready to Live: Prepared to Die: A Provocative Guide to the Rest of Your Life.* Wheaton, IL: Harold Shaw Publishers, 2000.

Levitt, Jo Ann, Marjory Levitt, and Joel Levitt. *Sibling Revelry: 8 Steps to Successful Adult Sibling Relationships.* New York: Dell Publishing, 2001.

Loverde, Joy. *Complete Eldercare Planner: Where to Start, Which Questions to Ask, and How to Find Help.* New York: Three Rivers Press, 2000.

Lustbader, Wendy. *Counting on Kindness: The Dilemma of Dependency.* New York: Simon & Schuster, 1994.

Marcell, Jacqueline. *Elder Rage—or—Take My Father . . . Please! How to Survive Caring for Aging Parents.* Irvine, CA: Impressive Press, 2000.

McLeod, Beth Witrogen. *Caregiving: The Spiritual Journey of Love, Loss and Renewal.* New York: John Wiley & Sons, 1999.

Mitchell, Marilyn. *Dancing on Quicksand: A Gift of Friendship in the Age of Alzheimer's.* Boulder, CO: Johnson Books, 2002.

Schweibert, Pat, Chuck DeKlyen, Taylor Bills (Illustrator), and Pat Schwiebert. *Tear Soup: A Recipe for Healing after Loss.* Portland, OR: Grief Watch, 2001.

Smith, Page. *Old Age Is Another Country: A Traveler's Guide.* Freedom, CA: Crossing Press, 1995.